DICK TAYLOR

WARPAINT

VOL. II

Colours and Markings
of British Army Vehicles 1903-2003

STRATUS

Published in Poland in 2009
by STRATUS s.c.
Po. Box 123,
27-600 Sandomierz 1, Poland
e-mail: office@mmpbooks.biz
for
Mushroom Model Publications,
3 Gloucester Close,
Petersfield,
Hampshire GU32 3AX
e-mail: rogerw@mmpbooks.biz

© 2009 Mushroom Model
Publications.
http://www.mmpbooks.biz

ISBN
978-83-89450-48-7

Editor in chief
Roger Wallsgrove

Editorial Team
Bartłomiej Belcarz
Robert Pęczkowski
Artur Juszczak

Colour Drawings
Mariusz Filipiuk

DTP
Artur Bukowski

Printed by
Drukarnia Diecezjalna,
ul. Żeromskiego 4,
27-600 Sandomierz
tel. +48 (15) 832 31 92
fax +48 (15) 832 77 87
www.wds.pl
marketing@wds.pl

PRINTED IN POLAND

Table of contents

On title page: A Sherman Firefly with a countershaded barrel - note the .30 MG

Get in picture!

Do you have photographs of historical aircraft, airfields in action, or original and unusual stories to tell? MMP would like to hear from you! We welcome previously unpublished material that will help to make MMP books the best of their kind. We will return original photos to you and provide full credit for your images. Contact us before sending us any valuable material: rogerw@mmpbooks.biz

INTRODUCTION TO VOLUME 2

In this second volume of four we will continue our in-depth study of the paint and camouflage schemes used by British army tactical vehicles. Chapter One looks at the period of the Second World War, a fascinating time, with many unusual and colourful schemes coming into use, including some short-lived ones that lasted for weeks, if not days! Much has been written in the last two or three decades about these schemes, but this has often been of a general nature and it is only recently that many of the orders and documents which gave the official line have been discovered. However, my usual caution must apply here - although there was always an official scheme in use in all theatres of war, many unofficial ones also existed alongside and instead of them, sometimes because of misunderstandings, at other times because of sheer bloody-mindedness! Roger and I have attempted, as before, to select many photos not only to illustrate directly the points made in the text, but also because they have not been printed frequently before. And remember that many of these photos contain a wealth of other information not contained in the caption - get out that magnifying glass!

Chapter Two looks at two related systems - there has been much confusion in the past about the geometric sub-unit signs used on British (and Commonwealth) AFVs, as well as the system of associated numbers and letters. My intention is to put this right, starting in the early days of WW1 and ending in Iraq 2003. I hope that this Volume will be as well received as the first, and that I continue to receive feedback, queries, comments and corrections from the knowledgeable community worldwide that I am privileged to be in touch with.

PAINT AND CAMOUFLAGE 1939 – 1945

INTRODUCTION TO PAINTS – SYSTEMS, SPECIFICATION AND SUPPLY

The whole topic of the camouflage colours and paints used in different theaters at different times in WW2 is a fascinating subject, and much groundbreaking work has been completed in recent years by a number of my contemporaries, whose work I acknowledge here. The tables at the end of this chapter summarise the main camouflage paints that were available to the British Army during the period 1938 -1945. Contrary to some sources, most of the paints used were numbered and named – the Camouflage Paints Specification Nos 1 and 2, and the War Emergency Standard BS 987 which replaced them both, stated by way of definition that:

> …by 'colour' is meant one of the official camouflage colours, which are described both by name and number and deposited at the Home Office…[1]

The major problem that a researcher faces when investigating these paint colours is that unfortunately the names were used both infrequently and inconsistently. Many unofficial and demi-official names were used. Decoding what was meant by 'Dark Green' or 'Olive Green' is more confusing today than it must have been when the original instructions were issued. Does it mean BSC 23 or 24? Or does it refer to SCC 7, 13 or 15? Almost in a tone of exasperation some orders from the period insist that demands for paint must include the appropriate reference number, for exactly this reason. The best clues for deciphering the names, as we shall see, are the date of the reference and the operational theatre.

Regimental histories and oral interviews with survivors are greatly affected by this problem, as we must often rely on verbal descriptions, with memories clouded by a long period of time; we must be very careful in taking such evidence as a literal truth. Light Stone is often called Yellow! And of course we are faced with the perennial problem of turning a verbal description of a colour into something more meaningful for our purposes. Also listed in the tables at the end of this chapter therefore are the various "Also Known As" titles that these colours appear to have been given, as well as a description summarising each colour's properties; wherever possible Red/Green/Blue (RGB) values have been given.[2] However, even during the early war years, complex paint specifications existed; for example this extract on the colour requirement for Paint HA0229 AKA "Paint, Prepared For Use, Dark Brown, Quick Drying, Matt Finish":

> …When applied to a non-absorbent surface and allowed to dry, a single coat must approximately match Standard Camouflage Tint No 1A.

Quick Drying meant that a second coat could be applied after no later than 16 hours, and that a second coat was required to attain the *exact* colour match.[3] It is most important to understand at this stage that the *colour* was only one part of such a specification.

A number of organisations were involved in the supply and specifications for paints, of which the War Office was in effect just the customer, and this was complicated by the establishment of the Ministry of Supply in 1939 to provide for the Army's equipment needs, and which altered the traditional direct War Department relationship with its suppliers. The interested parties included not only the MoS, but also the Home Office, the Ministry of Home Security, the Office of Works, the Paint Research Station (PRS) at Teddington, and the trade body, the National Federation of Association of Paint Colour & Varnish Manufacturers. The responsibility for the maintenance of the correct reference colours was maintained between the British Standards Institution (BSI) and the National Federation as the body representing the trade. The Paint Research Station was also involved in the maintenance of standards and specifications for camouflage paints, as we shall see. A system of standardised paint colours had not existed in Britain until 1925, before that date there was no central and agreed method of specifying paint performance, colour etc – this makes the investigation of colours pre 1925 almost impossible, as noted in Volume 1. After that date, BSI standards were used, the two main ones that concern camouflage and military paints were the colour charts for BS 381C first issued in 1930, and BS 987C, issued in 1942 but in use for at least two years earlier. Both were subject to amendments. (Private companies also published their own colour charts, such as Nobel's and ICI)

The Paint Research Station, Waldegrave Road, Teddington.

BS 381C "Colours for Ready-Mixed Paints" was the earlier of the two standards being initially available in 1930, with an amendment due to added colours in 1931; it remains (with many subsequent amendments up to 1996) the standard still in use by the Army today! The colours in this system were named, including colour names such as Portland Stone, Post Office Red, and Salmon Pink. Many of these names are still in use today.

The later BS 987C was issued in 1942 due to wartime necessity; originally it was referred to as the Civil Defence Camouflage Establishment (CDCE) specification. It was changed into a "War Emergency British Standard" in 1942 as a more coherent way of expressing the requirements for both manufacturers and users. The naming of the colours in this system was a lot less clear. For example, in a list dated December 1939, of the sixteen colours three are just referred to as Brown, three are called Grey, there are two Reds and no less than four simply entitled Green! The only useful (individual and descriptive) names are Tile Red, Pale Brick, Fawn and Black.

The number of colours in the CDCE/987C range did not stay fixed. In December 1939 16 shades were in use, the reference numbers being called "Shade Card Numbers". By May 1941 there were 18 colours in the system (1A and 4A having been added), and by then (actually from November 1940) these were being referred to as Standard Camouflage Colours (SCC), with the ultimate reference card, the so-called "museum set colorimetrically standardised", held at the PRS. The Home Office also held its own reference charts, the duplication probably necessary in case

of destruction by bombing. The colour cards sent out to manufacturers for their use were firstly checked against the master set, and if they were within agreed tolerances (ie the opinion of the checker!) then they could be used. This led to variations at two levels – the check of the manufacturer's card against the master card, and then the check of the paint produced against that card. (Prior to the adoption of this system in 1941 the variations were apparently much more noticeable, hence the introduction of the new method.)

In August 1941 the number of colours was reduced to 17. A second reduction was attempted initially in March 1942 - it was pointed out by the manufacturers that 80% of the paint they were asked to make covered only three of the colours – Nos 2, 7 and 14. It was proposed that these be retained as "basic shades" with five others retained for "exceptional use" (these were Nos 6, 8, 10, 11 & 13), with all the others being discarded. The proposal was not agreed and the 17 colours remained, although they were reduced to 11 later that year, probably around August. These colours were Numbers 1A, 2, 4, 5, 7, 10, 11A, 11B, 12, 13 and 14. The really interesting inclusion is 11B, AKA Desert Pink. As will be seen later, the first hint of this colour being used in North Africa was dated September 1942, and yet it had suddenly appeared as an SCC in UK a little earlier! And when it *was* introduced into North Africa in October that year, no-one seems to have ever referred to it by the official SCC number, indicating that it was considered to be a local colour…very strange. Other colours were added to the system towards the end of the conflict, including numbers 15 and 16.

The colour *chart* for the range was available for manufacturers in July 1942, (at a cost of 2 shillings and sixpence from Messrs Mitchell Colour Cards of Sandall Road London or direct from the BSI at only sixpence each[4]), but the BS *specification* was not ready until September as the new 11 colour British Standard BS987C. With effect from 1st December 1942 the colour of the much-used SCC2 changed, with the new version being referred to for a short while as Shade 2(New). Unfortunately, we do not know how dramatic the change to the colour was, but it was likely to have been brought about by raw material shortages, and may have only been of a minor nature, but it was certainly significant enough to warrant the change of designation.

Exact colour matching was a constant problem, caused by inconsistent availability of raw materials. Immediately after the war the Paint Research Station issued a pamphlet detailing their wartime activities, in which the following statement was made:

Whatever the type of raw material used in camouflage paints, maintenance of the desired colour was a prime consideration and only reluctantly under the pressure of events did the authorities ultimately modify their colour demands to accord more readily with the supply situation…It was realised that real production and supply differences were being experienced and that it was unfair to insist upon precise colour matching. Moreover the colour of camouflage paints varied considerably according to the surface painted, and soon became altered on exposure due to weathering and the collection of dirt.

Additionally, 9 of the 11 colours were authorised to have a range of acceptable tolerances, covering shades which were either lighter or darker or more Red <u>or</u> Yellow <u>or</u> Blue <u>or</u> Green that the exact specified colour. (The two colours this did not apply to were Green No 7 and Black No 14). It can be seen from this that attempting to be too particular and precise about what a particular colour was is something of a fool's game – the fact is that whilst the PRS held the "Holy Grail" in the shape of the "museum" colour reference card, variations frequently occurred throughout the period, and the PRS, the regulating authority, was prepared to accept that. Additionally, different chemical compositions and pigments were used by literally dozens of different manufacturers, all trying to achieve a specification in which *colour* was only one part; the PRS encouraged this approach of "improvising, substituting and replacing". Accelerated ageing devices were made, to attempt to quickly age paint to 250 hours; but paint mixes that achieved this benchmark (again, within the relaxed wartime tolerances) might not last that much longer in real conditions before they began to deteriorate. Each of these paints would react, fade and decompose in different ways, so even with the relatively rare well-preserved examples which do exist, we are not necessarily seeing the colour as it was when first applied or even a representation of the "average" colour. And let us be clear about the realities of the wartime situation: if a unit or depot put in an order and were then issued with stocks of paint marked as SCC2 (for example), then as long as that paint was of a Brown shade the exact colour would not be questioned.

Lack of paint was a constant complaint and worry in all theatres – even extending into the 1950s. ACI 1058/41 of October 1941 noted:

> Under present conditions, complete painting of vehicles is not possible except during overhaul in Base Ordnance Workshops. During 1st and 2nd line repairs vehicles will be "touched up", but under no circumstances will indents be submitted [for complete repaint in the field]...The scale of paint allowed for retouching purposes is 10% of that authorised for hand painting with one coat of colours.

ACI 1598/42 of July 1942 also referred to the seriously short supplies of paint and said:

> ...the practice of units carrying out their own painting has led to waste...demands for paint will be limited to the minimum essentially needed to arrest deterioration and to give essential camouflage. The amount of paint desirable for camouflage painting may be limited by the supplies available.

It was forbidden to repaint vehicles merely to comply with a new regulation on vehicle painting. Vehicles were repainted only after major overhaul in accordance with the above orders or upon moving to another theatre of operations that required a different paint scheme. A variety of schemes, old and new, could thus be in service in a unit together. Uniformity was not often high on the list of priorities! And the staggering amount of 80-90 MILLION gallons of paint was produced in the UK annually in the war years - the quantities in use were huge, and errors and inconsistencies and shortages could all play a part. [5]

Albion 3 Ton forward control vehicles. (IWM ARMY TRAINING 14/25)

Let us begin this detailed investigation by looking at the patches of light Yellow-Green or Khaki-Green paint that can often be seen on the fronts of vehicles. This was gas detector paint, which reacted by turning Brown or Red if in contact with liquid mustard agent. The detector took the form of an irregular rounded blob of paint on a suitable horizontal surface, in a position able to be seen by the vehicle driver, at the rate of 4 Ounces per vehicle. If no suitable surface was available, a horizontal metal plate, known as a tray, was attached forward of the drivers windscreen for this purpose. To quote *"Gas Training 1942"*:

> *Detector paint on vehicles.* - The detector paint
> is applied to the bonnet in an irregular shape.
> It should cover an area equivalent to about 18
> ins. by 18 ins. and must be visible to the driver.
> (Forward control vehicles are provided with a
> special tray, to be treated with detector paint.)[6]

Motorcycles were to paint a blob of detector paint on top of the headlamp and onto the front of the mudguard forward of the forks – and they were only to use 1 ounce of paint! (ACI 1671/43)

The use of the paint was prevalent in the early war years, but as the threat of a chemical attack diminished, its use became less common, but its use can still be noted in Normandy and

A Carrier being recovered, with two splodges of Gas paint in unauthorised but practical positions. (TM 1430/E/3)

Gas paint applied to the bonnet in the correct manner – note that the Allied Star has been recently applied, and it is possible to see where the previous RAF roundel has been painted out. (IWM NA2118)

beyond. (It was still mentioned in anti-gas publications as late as 1951, and therefore may even have been used in Korea, although its use was officially discontinued earlier than that). The reason for the two colours of paint noted above was due to changing the colour in about 1943; the paints used were Paint, Detector, Gas No 1 (Early period, Yellow/Green) and Paint, Detector, Gas, Khaki, No 2 (Later period, Khaki/Green.) The low contrast between this latter paint and the vehicle camouflage could mean that in many late war cases, the paint was in use but is difficult to distinguish in photographs. Paint Gas No 1 appears to have been used in some cases to paint low-contrast Allied Stars on vehicles in Burma – see Volume 4.

GENERAL

One aspect of the whole subject of camouflage painting in WW2 that is often overlooked is that it was not that usual for crewmen to paint their own vehicles, except when in the field; for example, when out in the desert, when applying whitewash as winter camouflage or when repainting markings after an inter-formation move. New vehicles were first painted to the contracted specification in the factory. Generally speaking most painting after this, including the application of Formation markings, was done at Ordnance Depots or Workshops, with the result that in most cases, a reasonably high standard was achieved; moreover a consistency of shades within batches of vehicles being repainted at the same time was very likely. Many official instructions of the period do not specify paint mixes, methods of application or quantities of paint required; this is because the Ordnance Depots would already understand how to do these things having received separate directives and were using trained personnel. In those instances where units were expected to paint their own vehicles, the orders would give more detail of the application methods, and would also be used as the authority to demand brushes, paint and thinners. (These included the wonderfully named Brush Lacquer, Brush Fitch Hog Hair, Brush Sash Tool, and Brush Varnish or Enamel Flat!) Initially brush painting was the most common – in 1941 British Troops Egypt possessed only one spray system which was owned by the RASC, but later spray painting became more common, as it was quicker and more economical.

A Matilda II being painted by hand in the Rushton and Hornsby factory. (Courtesy Ray Hooley)

A Crusader being hand painted at the factory in 1941. (IWM D4479)

Egyptian labourers spray-painting the tanks of 3RTR in March 1942 in the field – the camouflage scheme is discussed later in the chapter. (IWM E9885)

Spray painting a Canadian Truck.

When units did paint their own vehicles, there was always a natural tendency to make life as easy as possible, and therefore rather than start a paint job from scratch, especially when paint was scarce, ways were found that made the job easier and quicker, and used less paint. (Of course, this approach could apply equally to the 'professionals' in the Ordnance Depots as well!) For example, quite often the existing markings, especially the tricky ones requiring sign writing skills like census numbers, Formation and Arm of Service markings, squadron/company geometric signs, bridge plates etc, would be carefully avoided by being painted around or masked - grease was sometimes used as a masking medium when spraying. With census numbers, a rectangle of the original base colour was often masked off or otherwise avoided; and with the sub-unit geometric signs, the area inside the shape was often left untouched, leading to a high contrast in B&W photographs. When painting disruptive colours, the tricky bits like sights, MG mounts and tool brackets would often be avoided, the painter consciously designing the pattern as hc went along to make his life easier.

The basic requirements specified to contractors supplying military paints from May 1938 onwards were:
– That the finish was to be Matt (ACI 175/38);
– That the finish must be gas resistant and be able to be decontaminated of chemical agents;
– Interior paints were not to contain high levels of lead, to prevent flaking and possible absorption.

The instructions and observations in this chapter should always be read with an important caveat: many 'B' vehicles[7] were *not* finished in a disruptive pattern paint scheme at all, being left in a suitable base colour; the army distinguished between those that would be used tactically, and those used in rear areas.

The interior colours of vehicles varied according to the manufacturer, but the two main choices were Silver (aluminium paint) or White/Cream. Silver was the specified colour in British AFVs from the 1920s until mid-war when White or Cream No 52 came to predominate - because of paint shortages - changing back to Aluminium around the introduction of the Comet and Centurion in late 1944/early 1945 (and then back to White on Challenger 2).[8] US vehicles were almost invariably supplied in White. The insides of doors and hatches were generally painted in the exterior colour, and open fighting compartments likewise – for example with Carriers or the inside of the gun compartment of Self-Propelled Guns. Box bodied vehicles were finished in a light (White, Cream or Eau de Nil) interior colour scheme, and these were often painted with a light top half in one of these colours over a darker bottom half, meant to be scuff and mark resistant. Tool and stowage boxes were frequently painted in Red Lead (Red Oxide) inside to protect from corrosion.

Making life easy: the dark disruptive colour has been applied around the existing markings. The 51 symbol on the front right wing is actually on a small suitcase!

A Grant ARV showing the inside of the hatch covers still in White. (TM 2878/A/6)

The inside of a typical box-body, with the lower half in a dark scuff-resistant colour, and the upper half pale to maximise light. (TM 1667/B/4)

A 500cc BSA M20 showing copious overspray on the engine and gearbox.

A less dramatic paint scheme on this renovated Matchless, with the AOS marking and census number on the tank.

Very small vehicles such as motorcycles and trailers did not generally use disruptive patterns, as their small size rendered attempts at camouflage largely useless. The main components of motorcycles painted were the petrol tank, mudguards and frame, but sometimes the paint was accidentally or deliberately over-sprayed onto the seat, panniers or wheels. Ancillary components were mostly left in bare metal, often Nickel, Chromium and Cadmium, all in a dull finish where possible. Sometimes, such parts were "coslettised", which was a matt black protective finish. On rare occasions though small vehicles were camouflage painted; the Caunter scheme in the Middle East detailed a two colour pattern for motorcycles (although it is not certain if this was widely used), and the unique Malta scheme was definitely used on motorcycles.

The theft of Motorcycles and bicycles during the war hit alarming rates, and in an attempt to stop this ACI 260/41 ordered that "Trade Pattern Bicycles" (eg not military versions) were to be identified by having the top cross member painted Red, but ATS owned bicycles were to have the front forks painted Red instead – as they had no crossbar!

During the Blackout regulations introduced in Britain in 1939, road traffic accident and casualty statistics rose

alarmingly. As a result, vehicles in UK had to have the lower edge of the bodywork, wheel arches and bumpers painted with a 2-3" White line, in an effort to make them more visible at night. Officially vehicles operated by the military were exempted from these regulations but as an ACI (256/40) had to be issued pointing that out, it is likely that at least some vehicles were painted in this manner.

Home Guard extemporised vehicles, basically any type of civilian vehicle pressed into service, generally did NOT obey the various official regulations noted below, at least in the first two years of the war. As a result, many fanciful camouflage schemes were used, employing whatever paint was to hand!

A typical home Guard vehicle and scheme! This is the so-called Tickler Tank, named after Colonel Tickler of Maidenhead, who had this built from scrap on the base of a Sunbeam car. (IWM HU 35925)

BRITAIN AND NORTH WEST EUROPE 1939–1943

MILITARY TRAINING PAMPHLET No 20 (1939–1941)

In June 1939 Military Training Pamphlet No 20 issued instructions for a new disruptive camouflage patterning, clearly reflecting concerns over the suitability of the current standard one-colour scheme in the light of the looming European crisis. The base colour was specified as Khaki-Green No 3 as already announced in Army Council Instruction (ACI 96/39 and Amendment 837/39) of February. (It was also noted that this colour scheme did NOT apply to Egypt and Palestine.) It was to be used with two disruptive scheme options, one of which, Scheme 2, used Light Green No 5 as the disruptive colour. This was very unusual - disruptive colours were almost always darker than the base.

Scheme 2 was the scheme that the majority of the BEF went to France wearing, the use of the alternative Scheme 1 mainly being restricted to Infantry Tanks – the Matilda I and IIs in the Army Tank Brigade. Scheme 2 shows much more contrast between the two colours than does Scheme 1, which probably explains why it became the preferred option – what is the point of having a camouflage scheme if the two colours used look tonally very close?

Both schemes were meant to be applied to all types, not just tactical vehicles, and example diagrams were included. It was instructed to apply the chosen disruptive colour in diagonal-horizontal stripes, but photographs show two main patterns. Tanks wore broad diagonal (though not angular!) stripes, similar in fact to the overall appearance of the modern Green & Black scheme. Softskins often used a slightly more imaginative version, with thinner stripes that would veer off in different directions.

It is well worth reproducing the pamphlet in full here because it will allow readers to come to their own conclusions and interpretations; as far as possible, the punctuation, emphasis and layout have been reproduced accurately:

CAMOUFLAGE –
DISRUPTIVE PAINTING OF VEHICLES
MILITARY TRAINING PAMPHLET
No. 20

Prepared under the direction of
The Chief of the Imperial General Staff

THE WAR OFFICE,   June, 1939.

1. General

1. (i) The greater area of upper light reflecting surfaces should be painted dark.

(ii) The sides, front and rear should be painted with a disruptive design in which the masses of light and dark are approximately equally balanced.

2. Disruptive designs for mobile objects must be diagonal-horizontal in general lay-out. Vertical lines should not be used.

3. Plate I, Fig.1. A vertical mass is more conspicuous than a horizontal mass when moving across open ground, as it is directly opposed to the horizontal plane of the ground, and is more clearly observed in its relation to fixed bearing such as a tree, wood, or building in the distance or middle-distance.

Vertical lines increase the apparent height of an object, but horizontal or diagonal lines reduced the apparent height.

Disruptive designs must be varied and, when possible, an individual design should not be duplicated in any one company of AFV or MT.

4. When AFV or MT in numbers are parked, or in movement together, the repetition of one design may assist enemy observation, particularly when aerial photography is utilized.

5. Great care must be taken back that corners and edges are treated in the correct manner, which is clearly demonstrated in Plates II and III and explanatory notes attached to them.

6. For all general purposes, two colours will be used (the original basic colour and one disruptive colour).

Instructions may be given for the use of three colours under certain circumstances, but it should be noted that the general principles of design and treatment now defined should be adhered to irrespective of the number of colours used.

2. Scheme 1

Basic colour .. .. .G3.
Disruptive colour .. .. .. G4.

1. Draw a line of disruptive design on side of AFV or MT with chalk. Get right proportions.

2. Repeat the process on top, front, remaining side and rear of vehicle, in order named. Concentrate on continuity of design.

3. Give further guidance to painters by daubing the disruptive paint here and there within the outlines.

4. The work may then be completed rapidly by four or more men working on different areas simultaneously.

5. If more than two colours are to be used, do not draw outline of additional colour until first disruptive painting is completed.

3. Scheme 2

Basic colour .. .. G3.

Disruptive colour .. .. G5.

1. Scheme 2 is designed to give a lighter tonal effect throughout.

2. The same principles of design will be followed as in scheme 1, but after the chalk outline of disruptive design is drawn over the basic colour, the area within the outline will be left as basic colour and not re-painted.

The area outside the chalk lines will be painted with a lighter colour as supplied.

4. Detail of paints

The basic colour (G3) is now known as Khaki Green No.3; it can be applied either by spray or brush. Disruptive colours are: -

(a) Dark Green No. 4 suitable for average European conditions (G4).

(b) Light Green No. 5 for very light backgrounds (G5).

These paints are supplied in a paste form and should be thinned before application by the addition of petrifying liquid or water. As a general guide, 2 to 3 gallons of liquid are required to thin one cwt. of paste.

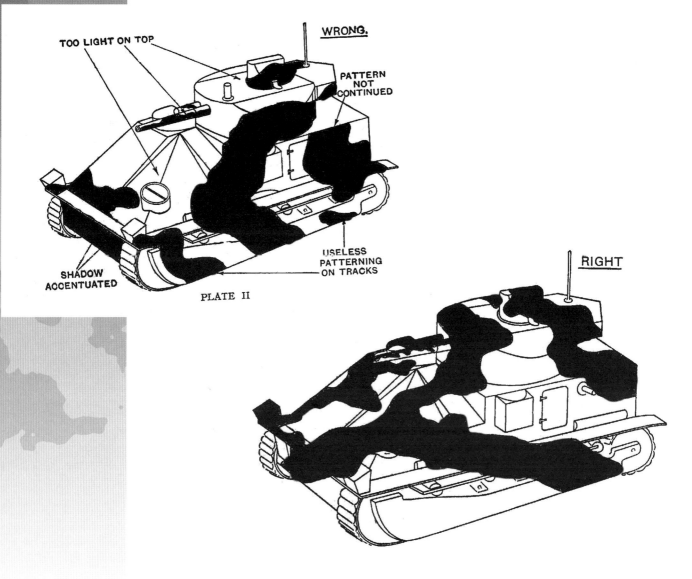

PLATE II

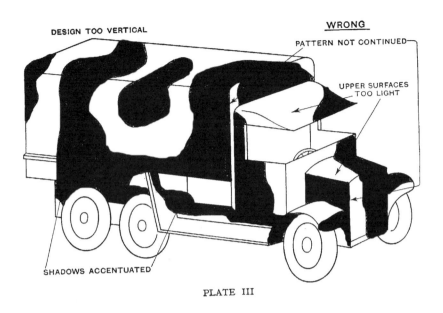

DESIGN TOO VERTICAL

WRONG

PATTERN NOT CONTINUED

UPPER SURFACES TOO LIGHT

SHADOWS ACCENTUATED

PLATE III

PLATE III.—*Continued*

RIGHT

MTP 20 PLATE I Side view of Medium Tank.

Matilda II in MTP 20 Scheme 1 – the tank has been captured, hence the Wehrmacht numberplate on the wing! (TM 241/E/6)

A Bedford 3 Tonner being painted in an MTP20 Scheme in 1939; the dark disruptive colour is probably G4; note how dark it appears when wet. The painters are working to the pattern chalked on the vehicle with the crosses showing which area to fill in with paint, as the instructions suggested. (IWM H800)

Light Tanks in August 1940 using MTP 20 Scheme 2. (TM 1595/A/1)

An A9 ICS of 3RTR in MTP 20 Scheme 2. (TM 3478/B/5)

It should be noted that MTP 20 explicitly forbade the copying of patterns within units, but some manufacturers or depots used what were in effect very similar if not exact patterns for the vehicles they painted – this may have been deliberate policy, or purely that the spray team responsible for hundreds of vehicles found it easier that way. Note that the instructions also authorised the use of a third colour "under certain circumstances" (which were not stated), but which was only rarely done in practice. Some Carriers in France in 1940 may have been painted in G3, G4 and G5 stripes, and an intriguing photograph of a number of 1st Canadian Corps vehicles in early 1942 show the two Green colours of Scheme 2 separated by thin (c2-3") irregular lines in a very light colour, but these were rare exceptions.

MTP20 patterns on BEF vehicles viewed from above; note how similar to the modern scheme the patterns are. (IWM F2312)

An imaginative version of MTP20, nearly Mickey Mouse! (TM 1679/B/2)

MTP 20 scheme on a 15Cwt Portee. Notice not only the different shades on the body and the canvas, but also the huge blob of gas detector paint on the bonnet! (IWM F2169)

The difference between Scheme 1 and 2 is well illustrated by the advice given in Section 3 Paragraph 2. Shown below are two identical tanks, both with an original base of G3 applied using the diagram shown in Plate 1 as the basis. The same patterns are used, but when the disruptive paint is applied, the overall effect looks totally different, as does the common colour G3!

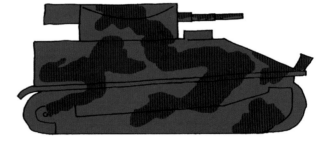

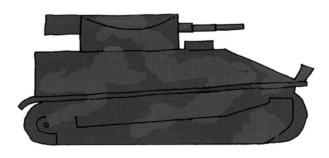

Military Training Pamphlet No 26 "Notes on Camouflage and Concealment" was also issued in 1939, and mentioned the painting of vehicles but dealt mainly with methods of camouflage and concealment, and described and authorised the use of "scrimmed" camouflage nets attached to vehicles, a system which was in widespread use by Normandy 1944. (MTP 26 was later superseded by "Vehicle Marking 1943")

This Albion 3 Ton is in an MTP 20 scheme using a rare third colour, tonally somewhere between the darkest and lightest, seemingly applied by patch painting. Note the difference in tone between the lightest colours on the body and on the canvas. (TM 1715/D/1)

A heavily scrimmed Priest in Normandy 1944. (IWM B5766)

Army Training Memorandum No 25 of October 1939 referred to the final paragraph of MTP20 and noted that:

> ...it has been found that mixing water with disruptive paint for camouflage purposes is a very poor substitute for the proper petrifying liquid. Camouflage paint mixed with water washes out almost entirely after rain and to a considerable extent after the vehicle has merely been washed down.

This was clearly published as a result of poor paint jobs and probably user complaints, and one can imagine what the vehicles thus painted would have looked like!

A scrimmed 11th Armoured Division Jeep in July 1944. (IWM B6962)

MISCELLANEOUS SCHEMES 1940-1941

Whilst the vast majority of the BEF went to France in MTP 20 authorised schemes, a series of photographs of 8" Howitzers taken during the 'Phoney War' period shows that they were camouflaged in the field by the addition of (very roughly applied) Black stripes. The question then is whether this was a one-off, or did other units - and their vehicles - adopt a similar scheme?

AFVs in European schemes were often sent out to other theatres without first repainting them. This Carrier looks conspicuous alongside its Caunter counterparts in Egypt.

A very unusual thin striped pattern on what is described as 'a 4 inch mobile gun' in July 1940. (IWM H2607)

CANVAS CANOPIES & TILTS

From the pre-war period until the autumn of 1941 the canvases for tilts and canopies were dyed (rather than painted) during manufacture in a Khaki-Green colour which quickly faded in use to a lighter shade.[9] MTP 20 indicated that disruptive colours were to be continued over canvas, especially onto the top of the roof ("the greater area of upper light reflecting surfaces") and although not explicitly specified in the text, Plate III confirmed that the pattern was to be continued over the canvas. No special canvas paint was specified at this stage. Either Scheme 1 or 2 could be used, although where softskins were camouflaged, the lighter Scheme 2 seems to have been much more common. In many cases, only the disruptive colour was applied, leaving the remainder of the canvas in dyed but unpainted Khaki-Green, and thus giving a continuity in pattern but a discontinuity in colour between the body and the canvas.

An Albion 3 Ton FBE Lorry showing a very dark canvas over the cab, with a lighter version on the side doors. (TM 1715/B/4)

C60L with the canopy from a different vehicle. (TM 1701/B/6)

25

MTP 20 pattern in
different colours on
the body and canvas
of a lorry and trailer.
(IWM H6271)

Two different interpre-
tations of MTP20 on
lorries; note how light
the natural canvas
colour is. (IWM H
4872)

Un-dyed canvas
overpainted with Dark
Tarmac, in contrast to
the body colour.

ACI 1559 of August 1941 specifically covered the topic of the **type** of paint to be used for vehicle canvases, and is reproduced in a slightly reduced form below:

Disruptive Painting of Canvas Covers and Hoods of Vehicles.

As paint, spraying, khaki green, No 3 and paint, spraying, dark tarmac No 4 have injurious effects on canvas covers and hoods of vehicles, the use of these paints for disruptive painting of vehicle covers and hoods will be discontinued forthwith.

In future, the following paints will be used for the disruptive painting of canvas covers and hoods of vehicles, and demands will be submitted as necessary through the D.A.C.O.S. of the Formation.

Section H-1 Paint camouflage bituminous emulsion
Catalogue No. HA
No 6188 Standard Colour No 1A
No 6179 Standard Colour No 7
The bodies of vehicles will continue to be painted with paint, spraying, khaki green No 3 and paint, spraying, dark tarmac No 4. MTP No 20 will be amended in due course.[10]

This ACI detailed not only a change in paint **type** for canvas, but also of paint **colour,** from the 'injurious Khaki Green' and 'Nobel's Dark Tarmac' used until then, to Very Dark Brown (SCC 1A) or Dark Olive Green (SCC 7). This order (just) preceded the change to the MTP 46 schemes noted below; note that the final paragraph still refers to MTP 20. This order would therefore have led to a situation in which the camouflage pattern on a vehicle body (for example G3 and Nobel's Dark Tarmac) would be in totally different colours to that on its tilt (Faded canvas with SCC 1A or SCC 7).

The very dark disruptive colour on this Morris C8 Quad could be either Nobel's Dark Tarmac or Very Dark Brown SCC1A. (IWM H8241)

Note particularly that Nobel's Dark Tarmac was to continue to be used on vehicle bodies. Continue? MTP 20 had not specified this colour, nor even suggested its use as an alternative. At some point between summer 1939 and 1941 this (non-standard) colour had clearly come into use as a disruptor, although the order for that change has not yet been found. Also, this ACI referred to two coded products called Standard Camouflage Colours (SCC), the chart for which was not produced until the following year. Clearly, colours were sometimes introduced into service prior to the issue of the charts.

Very shortly after ACI 1559 was promulgated, further instructions in the form of ACI 2202 of November 1941 (the same month that MTP46/4A, the pamphlet superceding MTP 20 was issued) were given, cancelling it and stating that the specified colour for painting "the top of hoods and the dark part of pattern at sides" was to be Very Dark Brown SCC1A, with a specified alternative of Black SCC 14, both of which were available as Bituminous Emulsions for canvases. Brown SCC 2 was now to be used for restoring the "basic khaki colour of the sides of faded hoods." The instruction explicitly stated that the whole of the top of canopies and hoods were to be painted in the dark shade, a practice widely followed and incidentally one which provided an excellent contrast for the Allied Stars which were later widely – despite being against orders – applied to the tilts of softskins as air recognition symbols.[11] In some isolated cases though, either because of lack of time or paint, a misunderstanding of the importance of camouflage against aerial observation, or simply sheer laziness, the disruptive colour was not applied to the vehicles upper surfaces, but continued up to the top of the sides only, leaving the roof uncamouflaged. ("The Sergeant Major will never notice..!")

From about 1942 canopies and canvases were dyed during manufacture in a darker colour than previously, designed to be similar to SCC2. This was to change again with the issue of ACI 1100 of August 1944, which ordered that tilts were to be dyed SCC 15, not SCC2 – to fall in line with the change in policy at that time – see below.

MILITARY TRAINING PAMPHLET No 46 PART 4A (1941–1944)

The MTP 20 instruction remained in force until November 1941 when, after it was cancelled by an ACI, it was superseded by *Military Training Pamphlet 46 Part 4A* dated 27th November 1941 and which was part of a series as follows:

1 General Principles 1941
2 Field Defences 1941
3 Huts, Camps and Installations 1942
4 Vehicles, Wheeled and Tracked 1941
4A Painting of Motor Transport 1941
5 Artillery with the Field Army 1942
6 Notes on Screens 1943
7 AA Artillery 1943
Supplement 1944 Prefabricated Dummy devices

MTP 46 PLATES 12 & 13. (with colour added) Adaptation of one pattern to different types of vehicle, using the Foliage pattern on a truck and a lorry. Fig 12 shows the use of SCC2 with SCC1A over; Fig 13 SCC1A over G3.

Fig 12

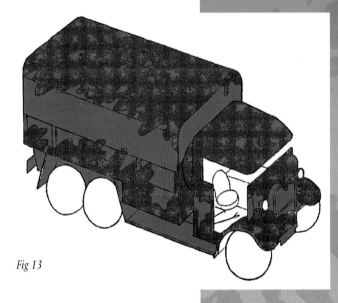

Fig 13

A Crusader in SCC2 in September 1942; note the style of the HQ 42nd Armoured Division pennant. (IWM TR154)

This Churchill is in SCC2. (compare the colour with the battledress), with a dark disruptive colour that might be Nobel's Dark Tarmac. (IWM TR 1409)

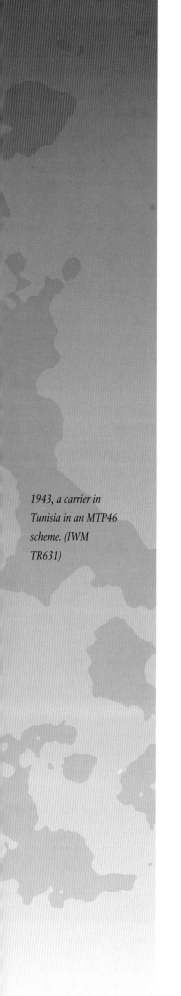

(Two others proposed in the series, *Concealment in the Face of the Enemy*, and *False Work and Deceit in the Field*, were mentioned but it is unclear if these were ever issued.)[12]

The title to Part 4 was a slight misnomer; it contained only one short paragraph on painting, and it was Part 4A which is the best source for vehicle camouflage instructions, although it does focus on B vehicles – there are no diagrams or patterns for armoured vehicles. The first six diagrams in Part 4A illustrated the 'problem' and then seven example patterns to be used were shown, and it was stated that:

> "For convenience, two colours only are generally used. For England and Northern Europe the light colour may be Khaki Green No.3 or Standard Camouflage Colour No.2. The dark paint should be Standard Camouflage Colour No.1A."[13]

As noted, the base colour to be used was now either G3 Khaki Green or SCC No 2 Brown - in fact SCC2 was to become the more common. SCC2 Brown was not a particularly dark colour, and it often appears quite light in B&W photographs; it was not as dark as many people suppose it to have been – the truly Dark Brown was SCC 1A used as the dark disruptive colour. Rather, SCC2 was a medium Brown.

1943, a carrier in Tunisia in an MTP46 scheme. (IWM TR631)

The main reason for SCC2 coming to the fore was not that the Army thought that Brown was better than Green as a camouflage colour, quite the reverse, but simply that at that stage of the war a compound called Chromium (sometimes referred to as Chromic) Oxide which was used to make Green pigmentations was in short supply, and the RAF had priority use of those stocks that existed. According to a report from the Paint Research Station in Teddington, "This pigment covers the whole range of camouflage green colours better than any other pigment or pigments, with good infra-red reflectivity and general colour stability...The successful substitution of chromium greens, particularly in view of the enormous quantities of green camouflage paint now demanded, is probably the most difficult single pigment problem presented during the war."[14] To alleviate the problems caused by the lack of the pigment, the Paint Research Station discovered that mixes of Yellow and Black pigments could be used to make dull green colours, and Yellow and Monastral Blue likewise for brighter greens. It may be that these mixes were later employed to restart the production of green hues of camouflage paints.[15]

MTP46/4A suggested examples of three distinct variations of solutions to the problem, stressed that they were guides only, and called these the Foliage Pattern, the Dappled Pattern and the Dry Brush Pattern. A document called "Camouflage Chart No 15" is often referred to in instructions from the period, and may have either reproduced the MTP46/4A diagrams of these patterns in poster form, or may have covered AFVs and/or B vehicles.

Crusader I. (or II) in a two-colour scheme; it is impossible to tell if this is the Green G3 or the Brown SCC2 base. (TM 4739/A/2)

THE FOLIAGE PATTERN

This name was applied to one of the three methods of applying the dark disruptive colour from MTP 46/4A, as it was quite distinctively different to those used with MTP 20. The earlier scheme it will be remembered was very reminiscent of the modern Army patterns, with broad diagonal wavy stripes across the vehicle. The MTP 46/4A Foliage pattern applied the same principles differently. ALL of the roof/horizontal surfaces were in the dark colour, and this extended downwards in a series of rounded peaks, resembling waves. Another series of these dark peaks extended upwards from the deep shadow areas under the body, suspension and wheel arches, leaving a band of the base colour running through the centre of the vehicle.

A probably unforeseen side-effect of the application of the Foliage pattern occurred with very small vehicles, like Carriers and Dingos. The dark patterning came to dominate almost the whole of the vehicle, so that there were only small irregular areas of the base colour sandwiched in between! One source indicates that in 1944 C Squadron of the Inns of Court Regiment painted their Daimlers and Humber armoured cars overall Black! This may be a slight exaggeration, but does reflect the general appearance that these small vehicles took when using this pattern.

MTP 46 PLATE 7 *The Foliage pattern.*

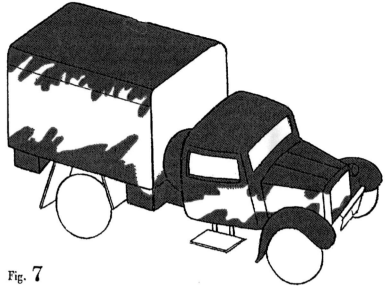

Fig. **7**

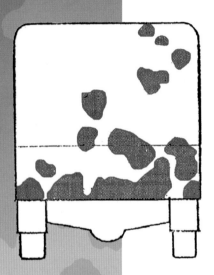

MTP 46 PLATE 8 *The Dappled pattern.*

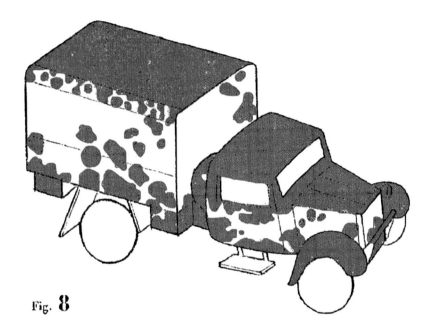

Fig. **8**

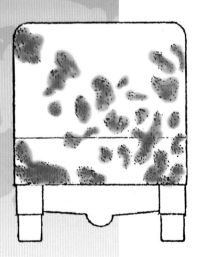

MTP46 Plate 9 *The Dry-Brush pattern.*

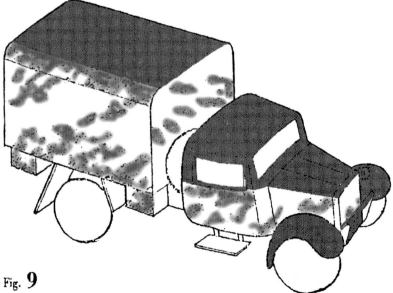

Fig. **9**

A perfect shot showing the wavy carrier scheme. (IWM H22720)

A Universal Carrier fording, in the typical wavy scheme. (TM1425/E/6)

THE DAPPLED (OR MICKEY MOUSE) PATTERN

One of the best-known variants of the MTP 46/4A pattern was the commonly but unofficially named "Mickey Mouse" or "Mickey Mouse's Ear". This was clearly based on the Dappled pattern, which showed a series of rounded blobs and blotches. With the Mickey Mouse pattern, the dark disruptive colour was painted using a number of overlapping circles of different diameters, and the pattern was placed around prominent areas of shadow, like the chassis, wheel arches and windows, with the intention of concealing the shadow. In some cases isolated circles and blobs were also painted onto areas of the base colour – this was shown in the Dappled pattern diagrams. The upper surfaces were often finished in a straight line along the top canvas or similar, with this straight edge being broken up by blobs extending downwards.

This pattern was not commonly applied to armoured vehicles, its use on AFVs seemingly being restricted to White halftracks, scout cars and light armoured cars. Its use was also restricted to Europe. In North Africa, only vehicles of the 1st Army used European colour schemes, the 8th Army never did - at least not deliberately; the discussion of MTP20 and 46/4A patterns in this chapter refers mainly to their use in the North West Europe arena and neither of these patterns was much used in the other theatres, the Middle and Far East. However, vehicles already wearing these schemes could be, and were, dispatched to other parts of the world as replacements. Sometimes this was because of a lack of time or paint, but leaving them in their original colours would also give less of a clue to the enemy intent on noting a ship's likely destination. Do not be surprised, therefore, to sometimes notice these patterns in use in other theatres of war. The Foliage and Dappled patterns both lasted until the end of the war – a photograph in the Tank Museum archive shows a Mickey Mouse-painted Truck parked under the barrel of a King Tiger in spring 1945!

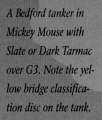

A Bedford tanker in Mickey Mouse with Slate or Dark Tarmac over G3. Note the yellow bridge classification disc on the tank.

Army Fire Service lorry in 'normal' Mickey Mouse' scheme. (TM 1673/A/1)

Bedford 3 Ton wireless body in Mickey Mouse with isolated spots. (TM 2589/D/4)

This version used isolated spots but did not paint the roof the dark colour as was so often emphasised. (IWM H24194)

This Generator Bus is also in a cross between the Dappled and Foliage patterns. (IWM H23874)

THE DRY BRUSH PATTERN

In this pattern the upper horizontal surfaces were all painted in the dark disruptive colour as before, but the base coloured sides were mottled with a subtle pattern by dabbing with an almost dry paint brush (or carefully using a spray-gun) so that the lighter colour was darkened, again mainly around the areas of shadow. This last example from MTP46/4A was apparently not much used in practice – it is likely that Commands and Formations instructed their units to adopt only one of the patterns, even specifying which examples from the pamphlet to use, and that the dry brush pattern was not thus specified.

Is this the very rare Drybrush scheme in use on this Austin K5? Close examination of the original shows the use of two dark colours, one of which appears to have been lightly mottled over the original colour. (TM 1685/A5)

MISCELLANEOUS

An extract of orders from the HQ Canadian 4th Armoured Brigade dated September 1943 gave instructions on the painting of MT vehicles, and conveniently adds detail to how a formation might interpret the general thrust of MTP 46/4A:

```
10. PAINTING OF MT VEHICLES
(i) Painting of all MT vehicles will be carried out strictly in accordance with
"Military Training Pamphlet No.46 Part 4A Painting of Mechanical Transport"

(ii) Types and uses of Paints are listed below, none other will be used:-
     Steel and Wood Bodywork
     Basic: Paint PFU Brown Standard Camouflage colour (S.C.C) No.2
Special spraying
     Dark: Paint PFU S.C.C No.1A
     Canvas
     Basic: Paint Bituminous Emulsion S.C.C. No.2
     Dark: Paint Bituminous Emulsion S.C.C. No.1A

The basic principles contained in the a/m pamphlet are:
-        All upturned surfaces will be painted in dark camouflage paint
-        Dark camouflage will be carried along the base of the vehicle and into
windows etc in order to blend in with the contained shadows of the vehicle
-        The remainder of the vehicle will be painted with the Basic (Light)
colour
-        Paint used should not be glossy and should have a rough texture.
-        Oil will not be used for cleaning vehicle bodies under any circumstances
```

It can be noted from this that it once again stresses that all of the roof/upper surfaces of a vehicle should appear in the dark disruptive colour. Reference was again made in this period to the patterns shown on 'Camouflage Chart No 15', which apparently demonstrated these principles.

VEHICLE MARKINGS 1942 & 1943

ACI 279 of 1942 cancelled ACI 31 of 1941 and its associated Pamphlet, as well as ACI 511 of 1941 and WO letter 57/Vehicles/8271 (O.S.6) of 18th March 1940. However, ACI 279 also announced the introduction of a new pamphlet known as *Vehicle Markings*, detailing the main types of markings to be applied to vehicles, as opposed to their paint and camouflage schemes. Another ACI issued on 20th October 1943 announced an updated version of this *Vehicle Markings* pamphlet, and Supplement A to this version of the pamphlet, a poster showing two example vehicles, has survived and is reproduced below.

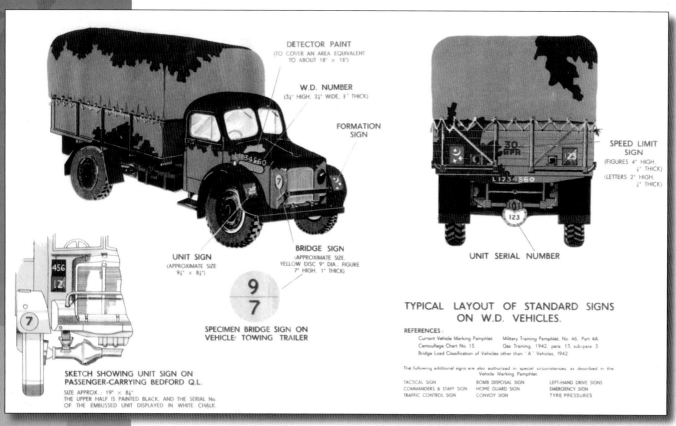

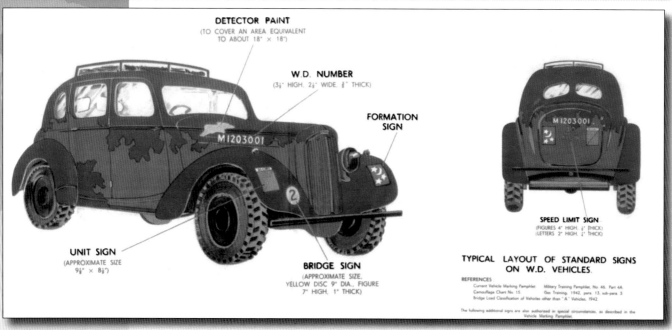

THE INTRODUCTION OF SCC 14

Also in October 1943 an ACI ordered that Blue/Black SCC 14 was henceforth to be the preferred dark disruptive colour, probably for reasons of supply rather than because of a deliberate change in colour policy. This brings us to the end of the mid-war period prior to the invasion of Normandy, and the next changes in the European theatre will be dealt with after a diversion is taken to look at developments in the in the Middle East and Mediterranean.

AFRICA AND THE MEDITERRANEAN 1939-1940

The vehicle camouflage instructions referred to so far in this chapter were only intended for use in the European theatre; for other theatres, the local Commands and Headquarters would issue their own orders, and the colour schemes used in the Mediterranean theatres were amongst the most colourful – and to the modern historian controversial – ever seen on British vehicles! As Alan Moorhead noted in "African Trilogy": "The desert offered colours in browns, yellows and greys. The army accordingly took these colours for its camouflage."[16]

British Troops Egypt GO 13/38 of January 1938 had ordered that all vehicles in Egypt currently painted in "Service Green Colour" were to be repainted with two coats of Middle Stone. Vehicles which had previously been painted with "Light Sand or similar colour" (presumably meaning Cream etc) only needed to receive a single coat of Middle Stone. Certain equipment including Tanks, Dragons and artillery equipment were also to carry a dark disruptor in the form of Dark Sand, in the ratios 2/3 to 1/3 respectively.

Issued on 25th July 1939 and also on the subject of special vehicle disruptive camouflage for the Middle East area, now clearly anticipating the start of the war, was General Order[17] British Troops Egypt (BTE) GO 370, which stated that all MT vehicles and artillery equipment in Egypt were to be painted with "Ground Colour Middle Stone" as the standard base colour, with camouflage patterning using a non-standard local colour called "Dark Sand" in diagonal stripes.[18] In effect then it confirmed the colours stated in GO 13/38, the main difference being that the dark disruptor was now to occupy no more that 20% of the vehicle. Ambulances were to be painted only in Middle Stone and were not to be disruptively camouflaged. Canvas hoods, canopies and covers were not to be painted, but the European shade of Service Green canvas could be "bleached and stained to light brown by [using] permanganate of potash."[19] Dark Sand was similar to the RAF Dark Earth colour, and refers to a local colour whose specification has been lost, and which had already been specified as the dark disruptor in late 1937 (ACI 648). The disruptive pattern was to be "brushed on in *regular* sloping bands varying in width from three inches to fifteen inches, the average width to be twelve inches. The total area of dark sand colour should not exceed twenty percent of the whole area." This GO remained in force until late 1940.

It should be noted that throughout the whole Western Desert[20] period (including Tunisia in 1943), the majority of 'B' vehicles used were NOT painted in camouflage schemes. They either used just the current base colour, or in some cases even remained in the normal European schemes, particularly if they were used exclusively in the rear areas. Once one of the suitable base colours was applied, it would be unusual for that vehicle to be repainted just because a new instruction was issued, so Middle Stone, Light Stone, Desert Pink and Portland Stone could all be seen in use as base colours at various times throughout the period 1940 - 1945 in the Middle East. Discretionary powers were given to Formations and Units to apply camouflage schemes to 'B' vehicles but only when their tactical usage justified it. In some instances at certain times even tanks were not painted with disruptive patterns, but these occasions were less common. As an aside, some 'B' vehicle crews were very concerned about the reflection from their windscreens alerting the enemy and thus invit-

Two shots of 44RTR in a single Stone colour overall, probably in Light Stone. 44RTR were in 1st Army Tank Brigade from December 1940 until the end of the Tunisian campaign.

Matilda II and Scammell both in Caunter schemes. (TM 1767/C/3)

ing artillery fire, so they often smeared the windscreens with grease and then threw sand on top, leaving just small areas for the driver and passenger to see through.

THE CAUNTER SCHEME 1940 – 1941

This famous camoufl age scheme was devised during 1940 by Brigadier John "Blood" Caunter of the 4th Armoured Brigade in Egypt. It should immediately be noted that the title 'Caunter Scheme' is entirely unofficial, but it is a useful and well-known shorthand phrase. The scheme was based on a three colour (only two colours on motorcycles and on some AFVs) geometric design with straight edges and, in a break with practice, with set patterns for different vehicle types. The apparent logic behind the design was that as more light fell on the top surfaces of vehicles than on the sides, by painting a darker shade over a medium shade over a light (base) shade, the tonal contrasts should be evened out, making the vehicle harder to recognise. It may also have borrowed something from the Royal Navy "dazzle" schemes applied to warships, which supposedly made it difficult for an enemy to assess speed and direction when moving and thus to engage accurately.

A Middle East GO of late 1940 (number unknown) cancelled the July 1939 GO 370 scheme of Middle Stone with Dark Sand and introduced the Caunter scheme, apparently after the 7th Armoured Brigade had conducted a series of experiments in May 1940. The scheme was to apply to the whole Middle East theatre, including West Africa, Sudan and to the Mediterranean islands (Cyprus and later Crete). A subsequent General Order, GO 297 of November 1940, referred back to this 'Caunter General Order' and gave the following detail:

- The new base colour was to be Light Stone. This base colour was to be common to all the Commands (These included Egypt, Syria, Trans-Jordan, Palestine, Kenya, Sudan, Aden, Cyprus and Crete).
- One or two contrasting disruptive camouflage colours were to be used, selected by the individual commands to suit local conditions.
- The disruptive colours in Egypt were to be Silver Grey (as the light disruptor) and Slate (as the dark disruptor). Green G3 was noted as the acceptable alternative to the latter.
- The dark disruptive colour in the Sudan was to be Light Purple Brown - in the wording this was the only disruptive colour specified, and meant a two-colour scheme was to be used in the Sudan; the Light Purple Brown was used as the middle colour, sandwiched between the Light Stone above and below.
- Disruptive colours for the other Commands were not detailed; the two above were mentioned only by way of example.
- Each Command was to specify which camouflage colours were to be used for the purposes of standardisation within their Command. (In most cases these decisions have not yet come to light.)

However, the final paragraph stated that the contents of GO 297 did NOT apply to: "...AFVs and Artillery Equipment which will continue to be painted in accordance with present practice." Without knowing the full detail of the missing original 'Caunter' GO, the meaning of this remains tantalisingly unclear, and we cannot be sure what this "present practice" meant. The pattern diagrams used did include both AFVs and Gun Carriages, and there are many photographs showing the scheme in use on such equipment, so it is likely to be a question of detail only. It appears from reading between the lines that what may have happened was that in late 1940 the original 'Caunter' GO changed the 'preferred' standard base colour from the GO 370 Middle Stone to Portland Stone, and then in very short order GO 297 changed this again to Light Stone, with the result that in practice Light Stone, Middle Stone (or possibly Portland Stone) could all be in use from then. Note that confusion with colours due to the non-standard use of names may lie behind some of these seemingly contradictory orders. Another detail starting to be seen at this time, which may well have been first specified in the 'Caunter GO', was the use of White paint to counter-shade the underside of the bow plate of tanks and other areas of deep shadow.

It would have appeared more sensible that the Egypt scheme of Light Stone/Silver Grey/Slate (or G3) was specified for all Commands, in order to make the transfer of AFVs from one to another easier – this was a regular occurrence. Unfortunately for the researcher hoping for a simple solution, this was later noted as exactly the reason why the Caunter scheme came to be discontinued.

Diagrams were produced for the following types:
- Cruiser Tank
- Light Tank
- Carrier
- Lorry
- Truck
- Gun Carriage
- Trailer
- Motorcycle

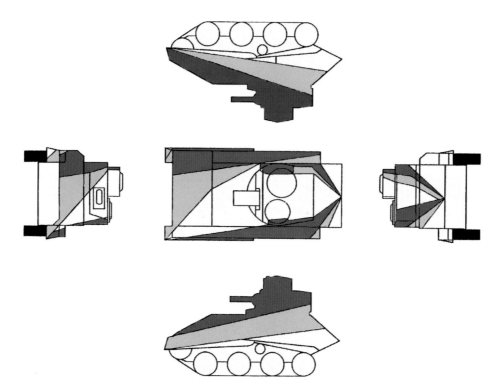

Shown here is the diagram for the Light Tank. It has had colour added to the original, using Light Stone and Silver Grey as the two lightest colours; the right side view (top) shows the use of Green G3 as the alternative upper colour, whereas the remainder show the preferred Slate.

In response to the request for listings of the colours chosen by the different Commands, British Troops Egypt issued GO 63 of 7th February 1941 "Disruptive Painting (Guns and Vehicles)". This started by noting the wasteful nature of individual Commands using different schemes, particularly when vehicles – as frequently happened – were transferred, mentioning in passing that paint supplies did not meet "present demands", and confirmed that Egypt Command would use the camouflage colours of Silver Grey and Slate (or G3) over Light Stone for their version of the Caunter scheme as noted above, and that in the Sudan Light Purple Brown was the only disruptive colour to be used. Furthermore, it advised that 3/5 of the surface should be painted in the base colour, the remaining area being equally divided between the two camouflage colours. Hoods and canopies were also to be painted in the pattern - this point probably needed clarifying because it hadn't been happening in the past, which would have undermined the whole point of the pattern!

The Australian Imperial Forces Mechanisation Instruction No 10 dated 6th March 1941 confirmed that the AIF would apply this policy to vehicles stationed in "Egypt and Palestine", but noted that "All AIF vehicles for the moment will be painted for use in Egypt..."[21] It then goes on to confirm the Egypt colours as noted above. This indicates that the Caunter scheme in Palestine *may* have used different colours up to that point - unfortunately the instruction does not clarify what they were. However, we do know that by August 1941 AIF vehicles in Palestine were using two particular colours, Dark Green over Light Stone, so this scheme had probably been in use previously, and may be the answer.[22]

Another highly revealing comment from Australian sources comes from the HQ DOS AIF ME war diary dated 18th February 1941. It notes that:

> There is no real check [i.e. quality control] on actual colours to be used for camouflage, and the present colours supplied are just copies taken many times by different local manufacturers. The result is that the colours supplied vary a lot.

In a similar vein, some crew memoirs from Egypt in this period indicate that they used a "Blue-Grey" colour in the Caunter scheme, which was obtained from a dockyard, although whether or not this indicates a Royal Navy colour is not clear. However, the RN colour Light Battleship Grey was similar to Silver Grey, and their Dark Battleship Grey could be used in lieu of Slate, and both therefore may have been used at various times due to shortages, etc. Some references have also noted the use of a Light Blue colour in the scheme and this has been suggested as an uncommon use of available paint stocks (Sky or Light Blue), and/or the tendency of the authorised Silver Grey to fade to a more blue-ish shade.

Vehicles dispatched from the Middle East theatre for the disastrous campaign in Greece in March 1941 were ordered to be repainted from what was described as "Hot Yellow" to "Olive Green"![23] Notes for units of 6th Division from HQ MEF dated 2nd April 1941 ordered that vehicles bound for Greece were required to be painted Green and Brown, but this order was issued only shortly before ships sailed and may therefore have come too late for many. The 4th Hussars had their Light Tanks (and potentially other vehicles) repainted after arrival on 11th March - in a Greek aircraft workshop! The colours used were therefore probably Green and Brown as ordered (and which were the exact colours then used on Greek aircraft), and were probably applied in a wavy disruptive scheme based on MTP20 principles. The photographs of knocked-out A10 Cruisers of 3RTR taken in the country clearly show them in a high-contrast two colour Caunter-style scheme, and it has been postulated that these tanks were painted in the Sudan version of the Caunter scheme of Light Purple Brown over Stone; partly this is because a source noted that in Egypt in January 1941 members of 3RTR saw their Cruisers in a base workshops "having their camouflage altered...to an exotic shade of Red and Yellow."[24] This happened, but was because a movement

A 3RTR A10 Cruiser in Greece 1941. The Caunter-style colour scheme is probably Green over Light Stone, with the Sqn markings in a brighter regimental Green.

order was issued ordering the regiment to prepare to move to Sudan, so the colour scheme for that theatre should have complied with this order. This probably indicates Light Stone and Light Purple Brown. However, whilst 3RTR's vehicles were painted in the Sudan scheme in early January 1941, they were then repainted in "Broad deceptive patterns of Green" in late February, just prior to sailing for Greece. The colours used were therefore one of the available Green shades over Light Stone. At least some of the regiment's B Vehicles though were deployed in the Egypt three-colour scheme.

Back to Egypt. In June 1941, instructions were given that during the vehicle painting process, sand should be sprinkled onto wet paint in order to reduce gloss and glare. This was later countermanded by Signal 4/105 of October 1941 because it slowed up the process too much; this same signal also cancelled all previous instructions on the subject of vehicle painting - see below for further detail.

It has been noted already that to some degree, Royal Artillery equipment could be treated separately from AFVs and B Vehicles. GO 795 of 8th August 1941 detailing camouflage colours (but not the patterns which were already in existence) read as follows:

> **ME GO 795 Camouflage of Artillery Equipment**
> Units holding equipment that has not been painted in Camouflage Colour before issue as in the case of Vehicles, Gun Carriages and Trailers will submit details as necessary to R.A.O.C. for paint of the following colours:-
> * Portland Stone
> * Silver Grey
> * Slate
> with which to paint the equipment to blend with the background on which it is normally used.
>
> The above applies to range, direction and height-finding instruments, predictors, telescopes and stands, machine guns and mountings and to cases for the above, excepting leather cases which are to be painted in service green colour.
> Care will be taken not to apply paint to working parts.

Note that the base colour for the RA was specified as Portland - not Light - Stone. This could be either a conscious decision taken by the RA staff for the artillery only, or because of shortages of Light Stone for tanks and other frontline vehicles. Also note that G3 was not specified as an alternative to Slate. GO 795 is chronologically the last known source detailing the use of Caunter schemes in the Middle East, as the scheme was about to be cancelled and replaced with new instructions.

POST CAUNTER SCHEMES 1941 – 1943

Allied forces in Palestine and TransJordan were already ahead of the game, having issued instructions to units in those theatres only in August 1941 to use only Light Stone with SCC No 7 Green as the disruptor, issuing example (non-Caunter) patterns with the instruction.[25] Canvases were to be painted in "conformity with the pattern". The ratio of colours in the diagrams was roughly 50/50.

On 6th October 1941 a consultation document in the form of GHQ MEF Signal 4/105 proposed that the Commands were to use a single colour only on vehicles, AFVs and artillery. It suggested that Light Stone should be chosen, but up to one disruptive colour could be chosen by the Commands. The use of sprinkling sand onto wet paint was to be discontinued as it took too long.

This signal was then followed by a confirmatory GO, 1272 of 5th December 1941 which read:

A 4th Fd Sqn RE. (7th Armd Div) Daimler Dingo with a small amount of dark disruptive patterning over Light Stone. (IWM NA1120)

A 6Pdr Portee. (the name BOOZY is on the shield!) in a two colour scheme, probably Dark Green or Slate over Light Stone. Note that the oblique patterning follows the general principles noted in MTP 20. (IWM E21493)

45

Late 1941 or probably early 1942: Stuarts in both Caunter and plain Stone schemes.

ME GO 1272 Camouflage – Painting of Vehicles, AFVs and Artillery
dated 5ᵗʰ December 1941

1.In future, all vehicles, AFVs and Artillery Equipment in the Middle East will be painted with a common basic colour. This will be either LIGHT STONE (British Standard Colour No 61 – M.E. Standard Colour No 23) or PORTLAND STONE (British Standard Colour No 64 – M.E. Standard Colour No 11), according to supplies available.

2. One contrasting colour may be selected by Comdrs to complete the camouflage scheme.

3. Comdrs will state what colour, if any, they wish to use in addition to the basic colour, so that a definite scale may be laid down.

4. Care will be taken not to apply paint to working parts nor to instrument cases made of leather.

General Orders No 297 of 1940 and 795 of 1941 are cancelled.

(Applicable to all Troops, M.E.F.)

Abbassia in Egypt, probably mid 1942 - a Lee, a Grant, and a Honey together in Light Stone. The A10 looks darker and may still be in Caunter.

The Australian Mechanisation Instruction No 80 of 8th January 1942 more or less repeated this, but also confirmed that Australian armoured vehicles in both Egypt and Palestine were to be painted in Light Stone, but without any disruptive colour which was only to be used in Syria, and that vehicles whose previous base coat was not in good condition or already bore a previous scheme, should receive two coats of either Light or Portland Stone. Care was to be taken that "markings (eg Army numbers) necessarily obliterated during the repainting are replaced, and that paint is not applied to tyres, working parts or instrument cases made of leather." This instruction again included pattern diagrams, identical to the ones previously specified for Palestine in August, but this time not specifying what the disruptive colour in Syria was to be; SCC7 is the favourite option.

GO 1272 thus in effect put an end to the Caunter scheme - although the repainting of vehicles that were already in that scheme did not necessarily happen quickly, even though the GO explicitly stated that all vehicles were to use the new scheme. A photograph of a Bofors being towed in Tunisia in early 1943 clearly shows that the towing vehicle was still in Caunter. Note that Light Stone and Portland Stone were the base colours of choice, but Middle Stone probably

A13 with Sunshield. (TM 254/D/6)

Crusader I in Light Stone with the centre wheels in Black for use with the Sunshield device.

The death throes of the Caunter scheme? This photograph, taken in March 1942, shows a Caunter patterned Quad towing a plain Stone coloured 25 Pounder. (IWM E9119)

25 Pounder in a plain Stone base, the original European base colour is starting to wear through. (TM 6307/B/6)

Bishop in plain Light Stone. (TM 1845/D/6)

North Africa 1942; a Grant in plain Stone, which has started to wear badly on the high-traffic areas, particularly on the turret top.

did still remain in use, however. Commanders were allowed to apply a disruptive pattern if they wished, but again the colour was not specified. Black, Slate or one of the Dark Greens would be the obvious suspects, but some research indicates the use of Light Purple Brown as well. As before, many vehicles, especially those not routinely at the 'sharp end', were simply painted in the base colour. It seems that as a result of this GO a large number of AFVs in Egypt in early 1942 were painted in a single base colour only. Tanks that were equipped with the Sunshield deception device often had the centre road wheels painted black and/or the sand-guards patterned, in an attempt to make the lorry disguise more realistic - this was particularly common on the Christie roadwheels on Cruiser tanks.

The seemingly endless streams of changing and sometimes contradictory orders must have led to a general lack of standardisation throughout the vehicle fleet, though not, it would appear, within individual Brigades where there was a greater degree of uniformity. From early summer 1941 on many unofficial bizarre and unsuitable schemes were tried, even down to unit level. Some

A Grant in the 22nd Armoured Brigade four colour scheme. (TM 2731/D/1

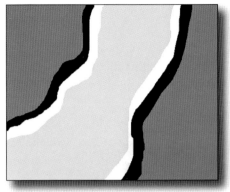

The 22nd Armoured Brigade scheme.

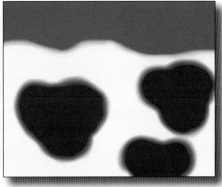

The spotted scheme used by 3RTR?

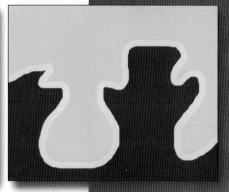

The 6th October 1942 scheme? The thick White or Grey line dividing the two main colours may be the reason why it was subsequently emphasised that hard edges to the revised patterns were to be used.

A Crusader I in North Africa, wearing an unusual pattern as a two-colour scheme, probably dark Green or Slate over Stone. (TM 1860/C/5)

The spotted scheme used by 3RTR in March 1942 – the darkest horizontal colour is probably the original US Olive Drab.
(IWM E9915 & E 9898)

51

of these schemes unwittingly acted as a means of identifying a unit or formation to the enemy. At some point in 1941 6 RTR were reported to have over-painted the Light Stone base on their Crusader Is with patches of either dark Green or Silver Grey outlined with Black. In mid 1942 the 22nd Armoured Brigade used a fairly unique camouflage scheme designed by a CLY officer in which a darker colour - it was apparently a locally mixed Brown shade - was applied over a lighter base (Light Stone or similar), with the Brown camouflage tone being separated from the base colour with thin Black and White lines. The scheme does not appear to have been officially recognised or sanctioned, and may well have been found to be ineffective or quickly banned, as it was only in use for short period of time.

Around the same time 3RTR used a unique scheme on their tanks that has caused much debate. The lightest colour was probably Light Stone, spray-painted onto the vertical surfaces but lessening as it neared the top to give a blurred edge, and leaving the top (horizontal) surfaces in the original OD, thus preserving a basic principle of the Caunter scheme. There is a third dark colour used as 'splodges', these could be Green, Brown, Red/Brown, Slate or Terracotta – anyone's guess is as good as mine!

This type of thing clearly had to be stopped. It had been observed in a report in September 1942 that there was

> an exaggerated idea, on the part of the army as a whole, of the efficacy of this or that favourite scheme of painting…at the time of the British withdrawal from Gazala in the early summer of 1942, [the] authority for Commands to apply their own disruptive pattern had somehow spread itself into a state of affairs where sub-Formations down to Brigades were designing and applying their own private patterns…when reinforcements were rushed [to Alamein in July 1942] one could stand beside the Cairo-Alex road and count every unit from Palestine and Syria by its own disruptive pattern.[26]

By this time GHQ MEF had already set up a camouflage directorate, which was headed by the energetic Colonel Barkas - he was the author of the report cited above - in order to solve the problem and apply policy at the highest level. In September 1942 the Directorate issued the GHQ MEF sponsored pamphlet "Notes on Vehicle Painting" which suggested some substantial changes as follows:

– Rather than the random patterns which (with the exception of the Caunter patterns) had been in general use until then, stemming to some degree from the basic principles outlined in MTP 20, each type of vehicle should adhere to a common pattern, for which drawings would be issued by the Camouflage Directorate.
– Reference was made to previous schemes used in January 1941; these were described as "beige and red-brown scheme for Sudan; a slate grey, silver grey and birch grey scheme for Western Desert, and another scheme for Palestine."[27]
– Research had indicated that a new "universal basic colour" was needed; this was described as an "earthy pink" and was to be designated as 'Desert Pink - ZI'.[28]
– The preferred single disruptive colour was to be "Dark Olive Green", but as before, alternatives could be used instead. These would be Dark Brown or Black shades. All paints were to be as matt as possible.
– The ground threat was viewed as greater than the air threat; thus, most 'B' vehicles would not require disruptive patterning; only those of "value tactically" would require this. Those that should be painted were "AFVs, Recce vehicles, Armd Recce vehicles, OP vehicles, ACVs, Quads and Matadors."
– Counter-shading in "dead white" was recommended, but it was acknowledged that it might later be "abandoned as not justifying the extra trouble in application."

GENERAL ORDERS

By General Hon. Sir Harold R. L. G. Alexander,

K.C.B., C.S.I., D.S.O., M.C.,

COMMANDER-IN-CHIEF, THE MIDDLE EAST FORCES

SERIAL No. 132	*4th December, 1942*	LIST No. 132

General Staff

1650. Camouflage—Painting of Vehicles and Equipment

1. This cancels General Order No. 1272 of 1941 and all Instructions or Directives on the policy of camouflage painting issued by G.H.Q., M.E.F., or subordinate H.Qs. thereof before the date of this Order.

POLICY

2.   (a) ALL vehicles and equipment will be painted in a single BASIC COLOUR common to the whole of M.E.F.

    (b) Certain classes of vehicles and equipment will be given an added disruptive pattern. This pattern will be common to the whole of M.E.F. It will be laid down by G.H.Q., M.E.F. (See para. 3.)

    (c) The object of the disruptive pattern is to distort shape, hinder quick and accurate identification of types, and hamper enemy fire aimed at known vulnerable points. It is directed against the ground observer and low flying aircraft. It will NOT necessarily aid concealment although in favourable circumstances it may do so.

EXECUTION

3.   (a) The BASIC COLOUR common to whole of M.E.F. is designated "DESERT PINK—No. Z.I." Approved samples of the colour and tone are held as controls by O.S. and the Camouflage Directorate.

    (b) The disruptive pattern will be in dark green, designated "DARK GREEN— P.F. No. I." If dark green is not available, black, very dark brown or dark slate may be used.

    (c) All paints will be as matt in finish as possible.

    (d) The disruptive patterns will be as laid down in diagrams to be issued by the Camouflage Directorate to O.S. under the same reference as this General Order.

    (e) The vehicles and equipment to be disruptively painted are:—

Tanks	Carriers, Universal
Tanks, O.P.	Carriers, Mortar
Armd. Cars	Carriers (tracked), O.P.
Scout Cars	Carriers, Wheeled, I.P.
Cars, Lt., Recce.	Self-propelled Artillery
Trucks, 15-cwt., Armd.	

NOTE.—A.C.Vs. will not be disruptively painted but will continue to be structurally disguised as at present and painted Desert Pink Z.I.

RESPONSIBILITIES

4. All new and repaired vehicles and equipments will be painted in accordance with this Order before being issued from B.O.Ds.

Commands and Formations will arrange the painting of all vehicles and equipments listed in para. 3(e) above, where these have not already been painted in accordance with this Order. Demands for paint and diagrams will be made through normal Ordnance channels.

Other vehicles and equipment will only be painted when passing through Base Workshops and B.O.Ds., or when repainting of the vehicles becomes necessary.

SPECIAL NOTE

5. This Order does NOT affect existing instructions governing the application to vehicles of roundels or other means of enabling R.A.F. to identify our own units.

(Applicable to all Troops, M.E.F.)   (CR/ME/42497/G.(Cam.).)

- Existing air recognition instructions - ie the use of roundels (see Volume 4) - were NOT affected by the new policy.
- It noted finally with regret that some vehicles arriving from the UK were still in "dark green and black."[29]

This report was quickly reinforced by a new General Order, GO 1650 of 4th December 1942 which cancelled GO 1272 and confirmed the new policy and the new colour. The choice of a pink shade may seem incongruous, but it was appropriate; Alan Moorhead described the desert as: "Level plains of smooth sand – a little rosier than Buff, a little paler than Salmon..."[30]

Pattern diagrams had been issued under reference CRME/42497/G (Cam) of 6th Oct 1942. Barkas's team then, for some reason, presumably to correct an error, almost immediately issued a new instruction (CRME/42497/G(Cam) on 19th October 1942 to the Depots responsible for implementing the order, ordering the 6th October 1942 versions to be destroyed and gave more detail of the new patterning, noting that:

- The general principle for applying the disruptive colour was to achieve a gently oblique sloping or horizontal pattern; it was NOT to run vertically.
- The disruptor was to "swallow up" the natural shadow and break up the hard lines where surfaces meet.

- More base than disruptor was to be visible.
- Hard edges were needed - no blurring of the pattern was to be allowed.
- Some counter-shading in White of naturally dark areas was to be employed, particularly under main armament gun barrels, under hull fronts and on the (non-disruptively painted) angled underside of Crusader turrets. This was also applied to the rear axle/differential on disruptively painted wheeled vehicles, and to the inside of wheel arches on Jeeps and other small cars. (A variety of counter-shading under the barrels on some US tanks was done by leaving the upper part of the barrel in Olive Drab or painting it in the dark disruptive colour, and painting the bottom half in a wavy pattern using the lighter base colour.)

The known surviving patterns are:

A/136   15 Cwt Truck no canopy

A/137   Marmon Herrington

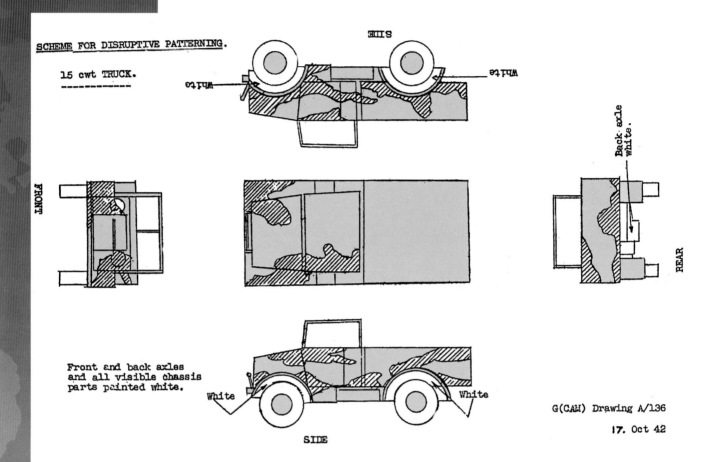

SCHEME FOR DISRUPTIVE PATTERNING.

15 cwt TRUCK.

SIDE

White

White

FRONT

Back axle white.

REAR

Front and back axles and all visible chassis parts painted white.

White   White

SIDE

G(CAM) Drawing A/136

17. Oct 42

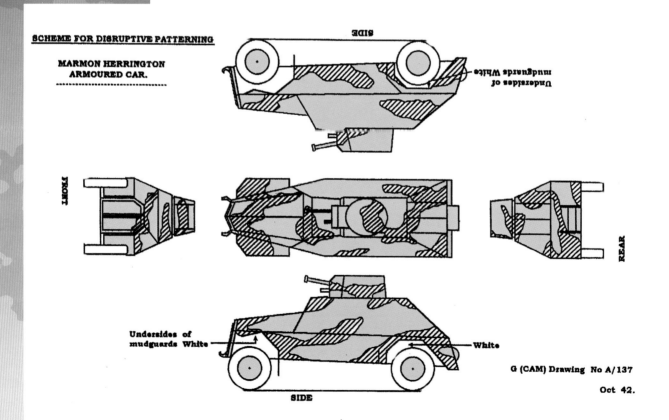

SCHEME FOR DISRUPTIVE PATTERNING

MARMON HERRINGTON ARMOURED CAR.

SIDE

Undersides of mudguards White

FRONT

REAR

Undersides of mudguards White   White

SIDE

G (CAM) Drawing No A/137

Oct 42.

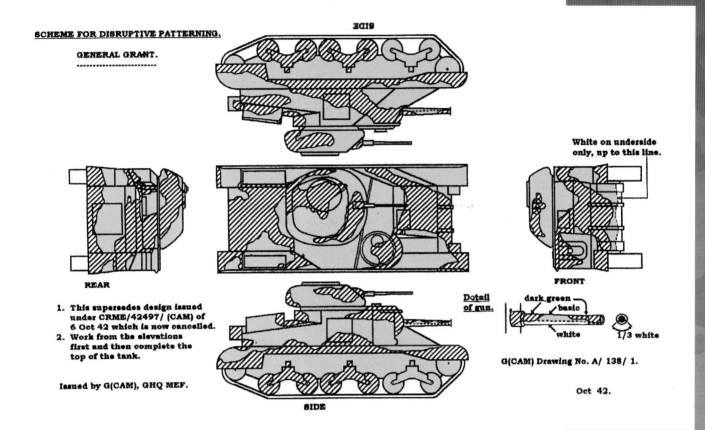

SCHEME FOR DISRUPTIVE PATTERNING.

GENERAL GRANT.
....

SIDE

White on underside
only, up to this line.

REAR

FRONT

1. This supersedes design issued
   under CRME/42497/ (CAM) of
   6 Oct 42 which is now cancelled.
2. Work from the elevations
   first and then complete the
   top of the tank.

Issued by G(CAM), GHQ MEF.

SIDE

Detail
of gun.

dark green
basic
white

1/3 white

G(CAM) Drawing No. A/ 138/ 1.

Oct 42.

A/138/1   Grant
A/139   15 Cwt Truck with canopy or box body

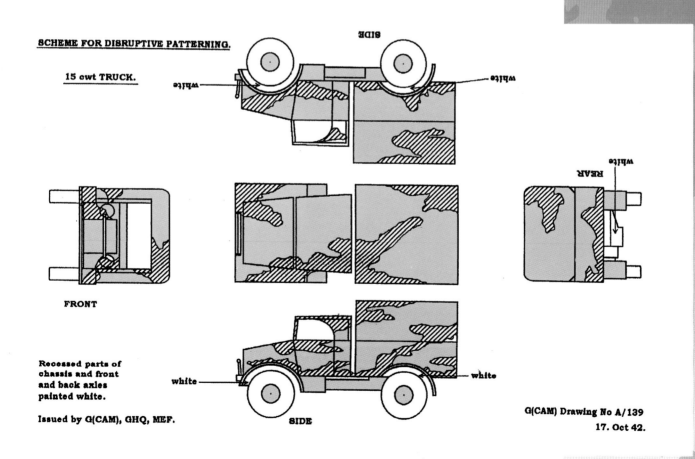

SCHEME FOR DISRUPTIVE PATTERNING.

15 cwt TRUCK.

SIDE

white

white

white

REAR

FRONT

Recessed parts of
chassis and front
and back axles
painted white.

Issued by G(CAM), GHQ, MEF.

white

white

SIDE

G(CAM) Drawing No A/139
17. Oct 42.

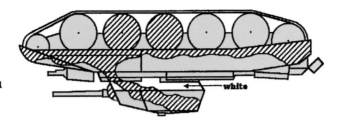

SCHEME FOR DISRUPTIVE PATTERNING.

CRUSADER.

(a) Recessed planes of gun turret·painted white.

(b) 2nd and 3rd wheels painted dark.

white

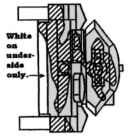

White on under-side only.

FRONT

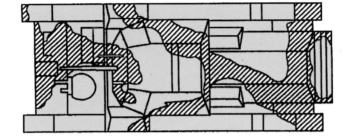

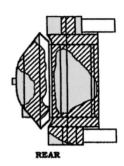

REAR

1. This supersedes design issued under CRME/42497/G(CAM) of 6 Oct 42 which is now cancelled.

2. Work from the elevations first and then complete the top of the tank.

Issued by G(CAM), GHQ, MEF.

white

white

1/3rd white

Detail of gun.

G(CAM) Drawing No. A/140/1

Oct 42.

SCHEME FOR DISRUPTIVE PATTERNING.

"JEEP"

SIDE

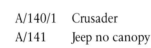

White

White

Undersides of mudguards white.

REAR

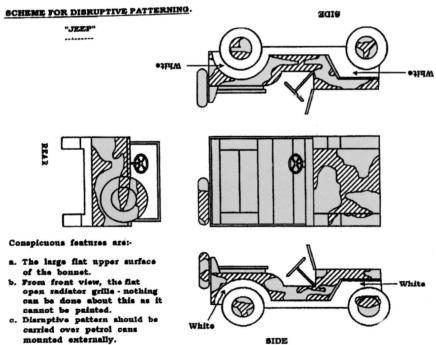

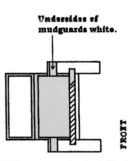

FRONT

Conspicuous features are:-

a. The large flat upper surface of the bonnet.

b. From front view, the flat open radiator grille - nothing can be done about this as it cannot be painted.

c. Disruptive pattern should be carried over petrol cans mounted externally.

Issued by G(CAM), GHQ, MEF.

White

White

SIDE

d. The spare wheel at the back should be absorbed in the disruptive pattern.

e. The pattern should be also taken over the dashboard.

f. Undersides of mudguards and the complete front and back axles should be painted white.

g. As the vehicle rides fairly high above the ground it is worth painting the wheels.

G(CAM) Drawing No A/141

17. Oct 42

SCHEME FOR DISRUPTIVE PATTERNING.

SHERMAN

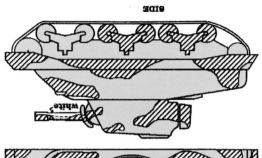

White on underside only, up to this line.

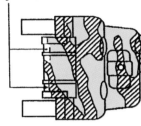

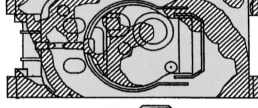

FRONT

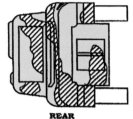

REAR

1. This supersedes design issued under CRME/ 42497/ G(CAM) of 6 Oct 42 which is now cancelled.

2. Work from the elevations first and then complete the top of the tank.

Issued by G(CAM) GHQ, MEF.

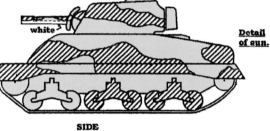

white

SIDE

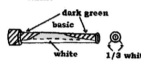

Detail of gun.

dark green
basic
white
1/3 white

G(CAM) Drawing No. A/142/1

Oct 42.

SCHEME FOR DISRUPTIVE PATTERNING.

GENERAL STUART.

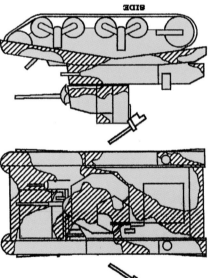

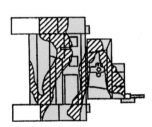

FRONT

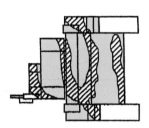

REAR

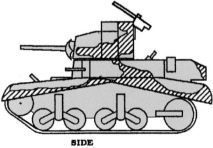

1. This supersedes design issued under CRME/ 42497/ G(Cam) of 6 Oct 42 which is now cancelled.

2. Work from the side elevations first and then complete the top of the tank.

Issued by G(CAM), GHQ, MEF.

SIDE

G(CAM) DRAWING No 143/1

17 Oct 42.

SCHEME FOR DISRUPTIVE PATTERNING.

VALENTINE.
....

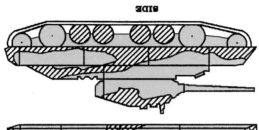

SIDE

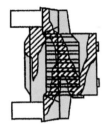

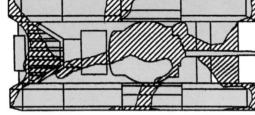

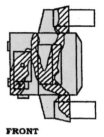

REAR

FRONT

1. This supercedes design issued under
   CRME/ 42497/ G(CAM) of 6 Oct 42
   which is now cancelled.

2. Work from the side elevations first
   and then complete the top of the Tank.

Issued by G(CAM), GHQ, MEF.

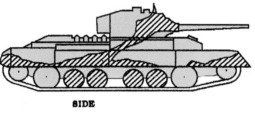

SIDE

G(CAM) Drawing No. A/ 144/1

17 Oct 42.

SCHEME FOR DISRUPTIVE PATTERNING.

MATILDA.
....

SIDE

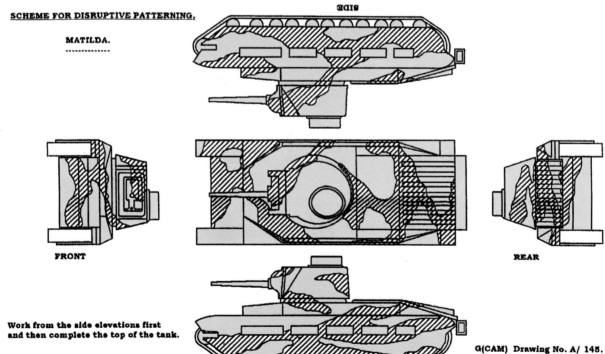

FRONT

REAR

Work from the side elevations first
and then complete the top of the tank.

Issued by G(CAM), GHQ MEF.

SIDE

G(CAM) Drawing No. A/ 145.

17 Oct 42.

The diagrams below have had the base colour of Desert Pink added, with the shaded areas representing the disruptive colour – Dark Green, Brown, or Black. Note that some of the diagrams specify the use of White for counter-shading.

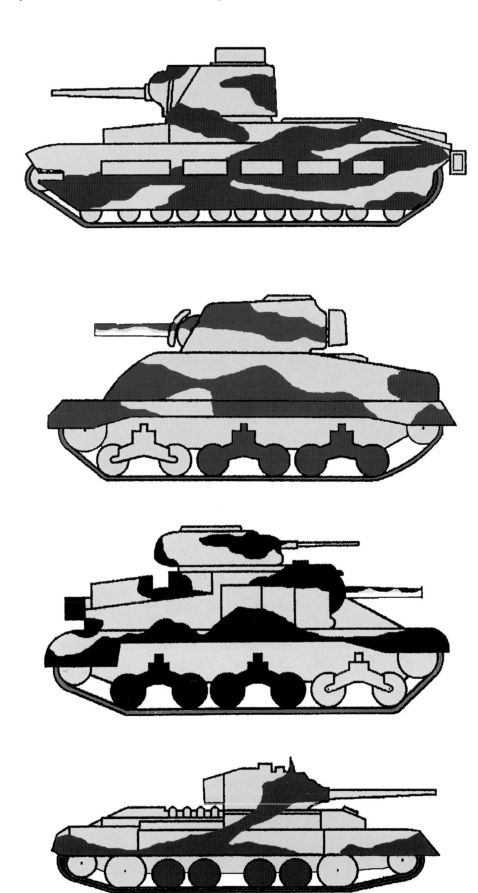

To illustrate the different 'look' that would result when the different disruptors were used, four diagrams have had the colours added; it must be stressed that it will be very difficult to be certain which one is being used on a B&W photograph!

The exact nature of the modifications to some of the patterns indicated by the suffixes is not known. It is a probability that, because of the high numbers noted above (136-145), that brand new pattern drawings always attracted a completely new code number, but where there was only a very slight alteration required to the previous version, the /1 suffix was used. This approach would prevent unnecessary repainting of vehicles where only minor patch painting was needed. Unfortunately, the standard military instructions to destroy all previous versions work against the historian!

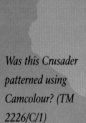

Was this Crusader patterned using Camcolour? (TM 2226/C/1)

Two other types of finish (rather than colour) are worthy of mention. One was called Camcolour, trialled in late 1941 and described as a "locally made camouflage paint made in the following shades: Milk, Cream, Sand, Buff, Pink, Terracotta, Chocolate, Light Green, Dark Green, and Black." It was mainly intended to be used on buildings, runways, structures and deception dummies rather than vehicles. However, an order dated 6th March 1942 confirmed that Camcolour could be used on vehicles "in case of emergency", and some photographs of tanks - Cruisers especially - showing especially heavy wear of the dark disruptive colour could well indicate this. Indeed, the same instruction cautions that Camcolour would not "harden unless mixed and applied according to instructions." Intriguingly, it then stated that "any shade...can be mixed with another to make special colours" – the mind boggles!

Camulsion (sometimes called Camemulsion) was a fabric dye used to impregnate canvas and material, and was therefore probably only used on tilts where patterning was needed – differences in tilt and body colours are frequently encountered, and one reason for this could be the use of Camulsion, as exact matches on different materials were notoriously difficult to attain.

The success - or otherwise - of the many camouflage schemes used in the Middle East is hard to gauge, but our friend Colonel Geoffrey Barkas, the 8th Army Camouflage Director, stated at the end of 1942 after the successful Alamein battle that: "*Camouflage had helped to put the fighting men into battle on more favourable terms, and so to purchase victory at a lower price in blood.*"

OTHER MEDITERRANEAN THEATRES – MALTA, ERITREA & SYRIA

 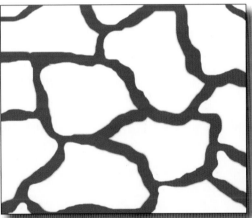

The 3 Colour Malta scheme and the more common 2 colour version.

Matilda II GALLANT in the earliest version of the scheme, using three colours. (IWM GM 494)

63

Light Tank in Malta scheme with a Maltese wall alongside, showing its effectiveness. (TM 1606/B/6)

The regular Malta pattern on a Station Wagon in 1943; the AOS serial is that of HQ RASC in a Division. (IWM GM3398)

The irregular Malta scheme on a Carrier named PYRENEES.

Another rarity which has become famous was the so-called Malta 'Rubble' camouflage, seen on most 'B' vehicles (including, strangely enough, motorcycles) on the island, as well as on the various tank types of the Independent RTR squadron.[31] This pattern consisted of a medium or light tone, possibly Light, Middle or Dark Stone, with a pattern of dark lines representing the numerous stone walls on the island, and seems to have been in use from around 1941. There were two varieties; one was an irregular pattern, whereas the second was more regular in appearance, looking more like brickwork than rubble, and often applied to B vehicles. Close study shows two different methods

It is impossible to be sure from any Black and White photograph, but the dark disruptive colour on this Carrier in Eritrea may be one of the Red-Brown hues. (TM 1419/D/2)

of painting the scheme. The first and probably earliest appears to have been done by painting blobs of the lighter colour over the darker base of UK colours, with a very thin Black line superimposed; the second a more professional finish using only two colours, often apparently Light Stone with Green or Brown.[32]

In the Eritrea campaign of 1941, Universal Carriers were employed in a very distinctive scheme, consisting of broad (about 6-9") horizontal wavy dark lines over a light base. The base was probably Light Stone or Portland Stone, with the camouflage colour being one of the Browns, Greens or, as has been reported, a Red-Brown shade, therefore Light Purple Brown, Terracotta or Red Oxide.

It has already been noted that Syria came under the remit of GHQ Middle East, and a number of armoured units - and therefore supporting organisations as well - were stationed there. The base colours used on armoured vehicles seem to have been one of the Stone options, overpainted with disruptive designs in dark Green similar to those adopted after the Caunter scheme was dropped. However, the disruptive colour used has caused some debate. One school suggests that from 1943 it was a Reddish-Brown shade, as the rock in parts of Jordan and Syria have a distinctive Red/Pink hue - witness Petra, the "Rose-Red City". Therefore the likely suspects are Terracotta or Red Oxide

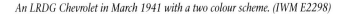

An LRDG Chevrolet with a darker pattern over the Stone base; probably Green. (TM 5170/D/4)

An LRDG Chevrolet in March 1941 with a two colour scheme. (IWM E2298)

as in Eritrea. Additionally, the use of Light Purple Brown has already been mentioned, and thus this colour may also have been in use. However, it could equally be a locally manufactured colour. This pattern may also have been used in Iraq and Persia.

The vehicles of the Long Range Desert Group used a variety of different schemes. The T, R1, Y and S2 patrol groupings appear to have used a single base colour overall, undoubtedly one of the Stone shades. In 1940 – 1941 the R2 and G1 and G2 patrols used Green patterning over the Stone base – roughly vertical stripes for the former and irregular blotches for the latter. From March 1942 both G patrols adopted a more esoteric scheme, devised by Capt Timpson and Lt Gurdon. This has been described as broad bands and blotches "somewhat bold...in pink, yellow and green... overspray blending them into a less-than-harmonious whole." This bizarre scheme is all the more interesting as the G patrols were formed from the Guards!

TUNISIA 1943

This is the 16/5th Lancers on parade for a Turkish Military Mission on 28th March 1943 in Tunisia. (IWM E23724)

Crusader III in Tunisia. (TM 1836/E/2)

When the Eighth Army drove westwards into Tunisia in February 1943, the terrain changed from the stark desert wastes of Egypt and Libya into the stonier and more vegetated Tunisian landscape. This necessitated a change of scheme whilst in the middle of a major advance. One source notes that at about this time the Sherwood Rangers Yeomanry managed to 'acquire' a quantity of Green paint, which may even have been in a number of different shades, and applied it quickly to their tanks, using brushes or even rags. One can only imagine the effect of this extemporised finish!

A series of photographs of a parade in Tripolitania (western Libya) by 6th Armoured Division show some of the Shermans with light coloured suspensions, but a noticeably darker base colour over-spotted with numerous irregular blobs of a yet darker colour - Green? Some of the other Shermans in the line up are in what appears to be an Olive Drab or dark Green overall, but again with light toned suspensions.

The vehicles belonging to 1st Army that landed in the 'Torch' landings and advanced eastwards into Tunisia were not desert camouflaged. They arrived in the normal UK MTP46/4A schemes of SCC2 or G3 bases, with or without disruptive patterning. They were to remain in these schemes until repainted ready for the invasions of Sicily and Italy.

MISCELLANEOUS SCHEMES IN NORTH AFRICA

There are always intriguing exceptions to the rules, some having been commented on already. There were others. In the Western Desert in about 1941, the 11th Hussars RHQ contained a box-bodied lorry, painted on the left-hand side of which was a huge coloured map of Europe, North Africa and Western Russia, which was used to brief on the war situation. In June 1942 some 25 Pounder guns and their limbers (and so presumably their tractors as well) were photographed with a dark dapple pattern (Brown?) over a lighter Stone base.

Kingforce Churchill.
(TM 1780/B/3)

General Lumsden, an ex 12th Lancer who commanded X Corps in the Western Desert in 1942 may have taken the principle of counter-shading too far! He was reported to have"galloped around the battlefield in his White-painted tank".[33] This story unfortunately cannot be completely confirmed, nor can the type of tank used if it is true (most of the tanks in his Corps in late 1942 were Shermans, but he may have used a Grant command tank), as no photograph has yet been discovered, but he certainly would have been readily identifiable and it does suggest a most unusual if not unique vignette.

The six 'Kingforce' Churchills sent to the Western Desert in early October 1942 for evaluation arrived in one of the European schemes, either Green G3 or (more likely) Brown SCC No 2 overall. They may also have already had a disruptive paint scheme applied in the UK but this is unlikely, as they were probably shipped out quickly, almost straight from the factory. When they arrived, they stood out like the proverbial and had to be repainted before they could be used. It seems that this was done at unit level, by the members of 'Kingforce' who operated them, and to a standard pattern of their own devising. The result was a rare example of where the disruptive colour was the lighter colour as it was applied second, and the tone of the available photographs suggest that one of the Stones was used.

SICILY AND ITALY 1943

Towards the end of the Tunisian campaign thoughts had clearly already turned to the invasions of Sicily and Italy. The scheme initially adopted for those campaigns seems to have originated from XIII Corps, when General Dempsey: "has laid down that vehicles will be camouflaged Light Brown [sic], disruptive pattern." It further appears that Dempsey himself personally approved the shade which came to be known as Light Mud, and that the paint was produced in Egypt, as units were told that the reason for delays in supply was that it was coming from that country. It is not clear however if the new schemes and colours were designed with Tunisia or Italy in mind.

On 10th April 1943 orders for new camouflage paint schemes were issued, and these cancelled "the recent ME GO 1650". In essence, the base colour was to be a new colour called Light Mud. Blue-Black SCC14 was to be the disruptive colour, applied in a ratio of 2:1 respectively. Unlike previous instructions, no alternative disruptive colour was suggested in the original instruction, but Greens 6A and 7, and Dark Brown 1A were all used in practice. A XIII Corps directive of the period states that this disruptive scheme was to be used on all vehicles, as well as on 25 Pdr Gunshields front and rear, and it can be inferred from this that all vehicles, not just 'tactical vehicles', were now to be camouflaged. However, some softskins and halftracks have been noted using the light base colour only, and some Churchills alone amongst tank types seem to have retained their MTP46/4A SCC2 schemes in Italy. A number of 'B' vehicles wore a variation of the scheme in which the Light Mud base was the dominant colour, with only small amounts of SCC14 used to add thin stripes, with tilts left in 'Mickey Mouse' pattern and in some cases not patterned at all. Later, on 4th June 1943, ME GO 693/43 was issued and formally cancelled GO 1650 and also confirmed the new colour as Light Mud. "Field Force" units were to have a disruptor applied, preferably Blue-Black, with Dark Green, Very Dark Brown and Dark Slate being the authorised alternatives. "Undershading" in White was still to be employed, and it further noted that vehicles arriving in UK colours were simply to have the Light Mud only painted over the existing paint. The order did not apply to vehicles in Sudan; by inference then it applied everywhere else.

Models were used to decide on the exact designs for the different vehicle types and which were issued dated 12th April 1943, this time with photographs of the models as well, and were, in some cases, quite different to the previous patterns.[34]

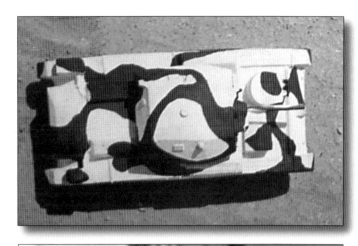

The model of the Crusader used to determine the A/188 Pattern.

The Grant model used to draw A/186.

Patterns that have survived are:

A/181   Sherman

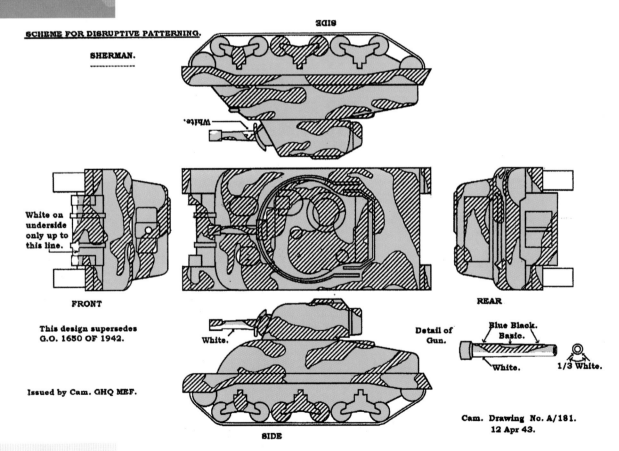

SCHEME FOR DISRUPTIVE PATTERNING.

SHERMAN.

SIDE

White.

White on
underside
only up to
this line.

FRONT

This design supersedes
G.O. 1650 OF 1942.

Issued by Cam. GHQ MEF.

White.

SIDE

REAR

Detail of
Gun.

Blue Black.
Basic.

White.

1/3 White.

Cam. Drawing No. A/181.
12 Apr 43.

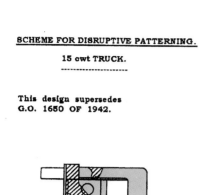

SCHEME FOR DISRUPTIVE PATTERNING.

15 cwt TRUCK.

This design supersedes
G.O. 1650 OF 1942.

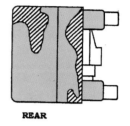

FRONT

Work from the elevations
first and then complete the
top of the truck.

Issued by Cam. GHQ MEF.

REAR

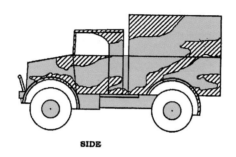

SIDE

Cam. Drawing No. A/183.

Apr 43.

A/183   15 cwt truck with canopy or box body

A/184   3 Ton Bedford

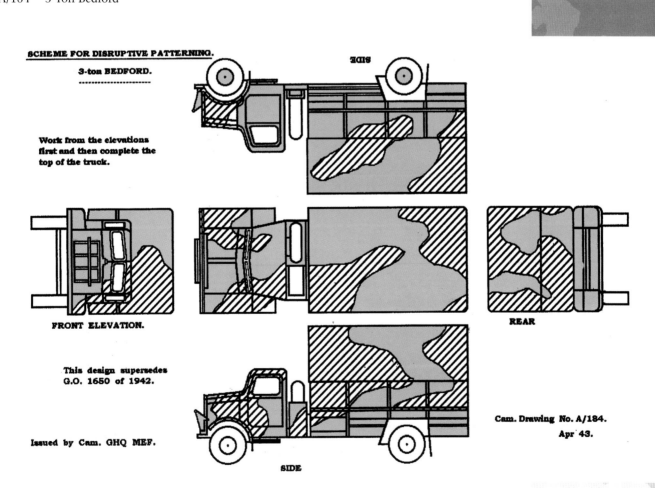

SCHEME FOR DISRUPTIVE PATTERNING.

3-ton BEDFORD.

Work from the elevations
first and then complete the
top of the truck.

FRONT ELEVATION.

This design supersedes
G.O. 1650 of 1942.

Issued by Cam. GHQ MEF.

REAR

SIDE

Cam. Drawing No. A/184.

Apr 43.

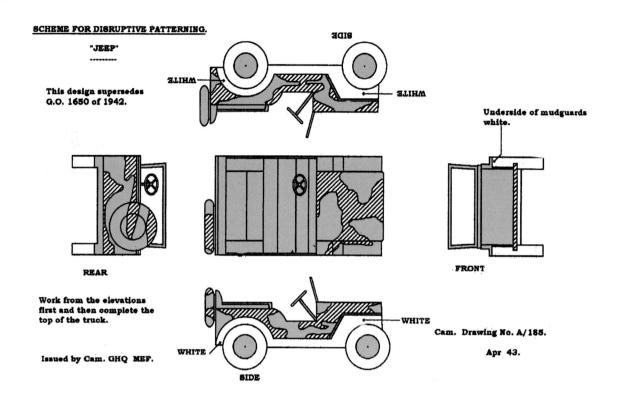

SCHEME FOR DISRUPTIVE PATTERNING.

"JEEP"

This design supersedes
G.O. 1650 of 1942.

SIDE

WHITE

WHITE

Underside of mudguards
white.

REAR

FRONT

Work from the elevations
first and then complete the
top of the truck.

WHITE

WHITE

Cam. Drawing No. A/185.

Apr 43.

Issued by Cam. GHQ MEF.

SIDE

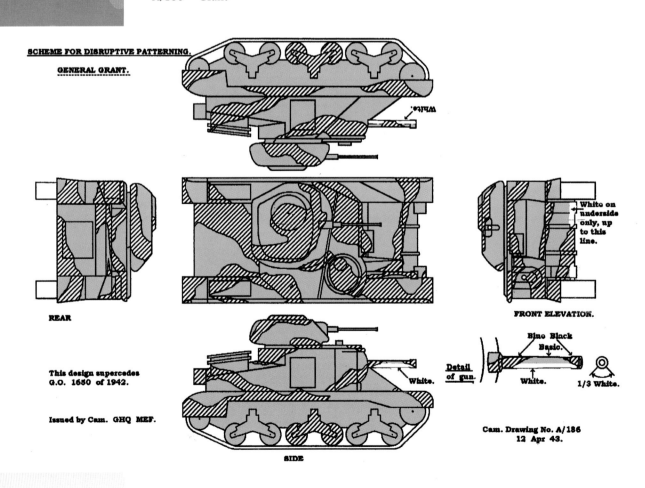

SCHEME FOR DISRUPTIVE PATTERNING.

GENERAL GRANT.

White.

REAR

White on
underside
only, up
to this
line.

FRONT ELEVATION.

This design supercedes
G.O. 1650 of 1942.

White.

Bino Block
Basic.

Detail
of gun.

White.

1/3 White.

Issued by Cam. GHQ MEF.

SIDE

Cam. Drawing No. A/186
12 Apr 43.

SCHEME FOR DISRUPTIVE PATTERNING.

CRUSADER.

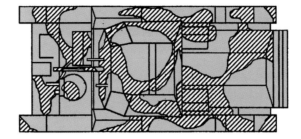
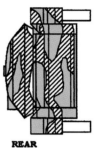

Recessed planes of gun
turret painted white.

White.

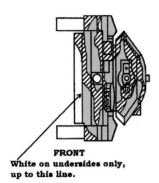

FRONT
White on undersides only,
up to this line.

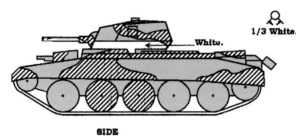

This design supercedes
G.O. 1650 OF 1942.

Issued by Cam. GHQ. MEF.

REAR

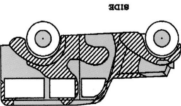

1/3 White.

White.

White.

Detail of gun.

Cam. Drawing No. A/188
12 April 42.

SIDE

SCHEME FOR DISRUPTIVE PATTERNING.

HUMBER UTILITY.

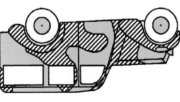

This design supersedes
G.O. 1650 of 1942.

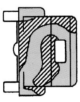

REAR

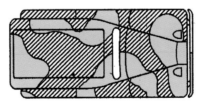

FRONT

Work from the elevations
first and then complete the
top of vehicle.

Issued by Cam. GHQ MEF.

SIDE

Cam. Drawing No. A/189

Apr 43.

15-cwt ARMOURED TRUCK.

SIDE

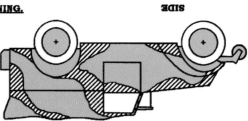

This design supercedes
G.O. 1650 of 1942.

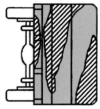
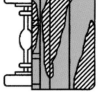
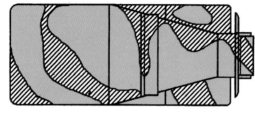
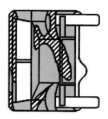

REAR

FRONT

Work from the elevations
first and then complete
the top-of the truck.

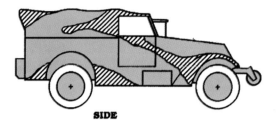

Issued by Cam. GHQ MEF.

SIDE

Cam. Drawing No. A/190
Apr 43.

A/190   15 cwt Armoured Truck (White Scout Car)
A/191   Priest

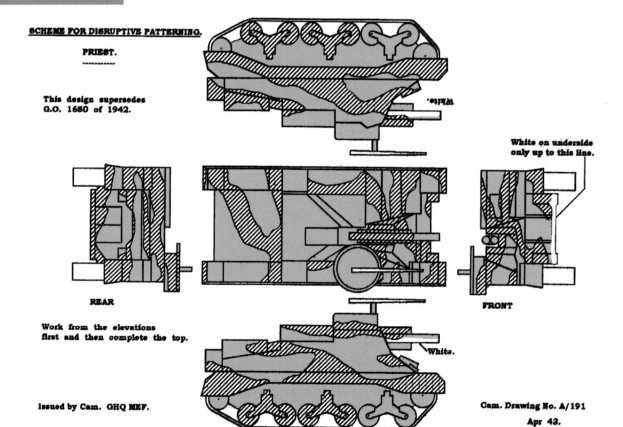

SCHEME FOR DISRUPTIVE PATTERNING.

PRIEST.

This design supersedes
G.O. 1650 of 1942.

White on underside
only up to this line.

White.

REAR

FRONT

Work from the elevations
first and then complete the top.

White.

Issued by Cam. GHQ MEF.

Cam. Drawing No. A/191
Apr 43.

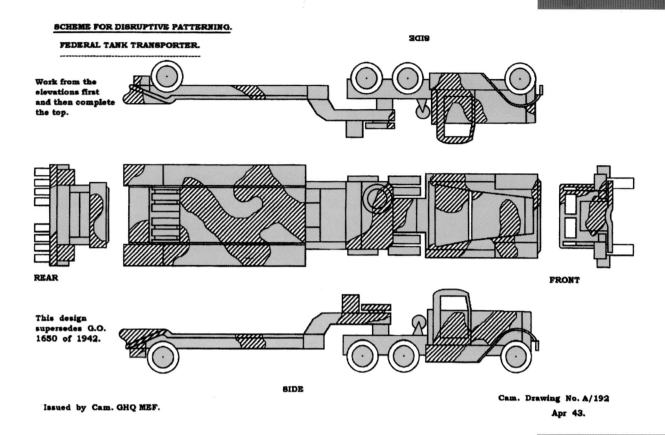

SCHEME FOR DISRUPTIVE PATTERNING.

FEDERAL TANK TRANSPORTER.

SIDE

Work from the
elevations first
and then complete
the top.

REAR

FRONT

This design
supersedes G.O.
1650 of 1942.

SIDE

Issued by Cam. GHQ MEF.

Cam. Drawing No. A/192
Apr 43.

A/192   Federal (Diamond T) Tank Transporter
A/193   GMC Light Recce Car (Otter)

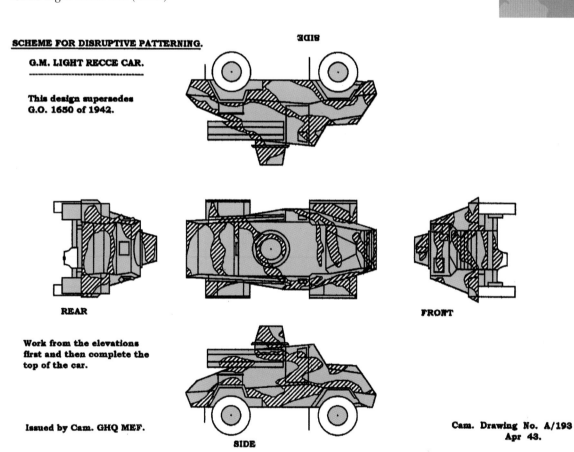

SCHEME FOR DISRUPTIVE PATTERNING.

G.M. LIGHT RECCE CAR.

SIDE

This design supersedes
G.O. 1650 of 1942.

REAR

FRONT

Work from the elevations
first and then complete the
top of the car.

SIDE

Issued by Cam. GHQ MEF.

Cam. Drawing No. A/193
Apr 43.

SCHEME FOR DISRUPTIVE PATTERNING:

BREN GUN CARRIER.

SIDE

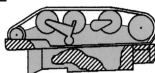

This design supercedes
G.O. 1650 of 1942.

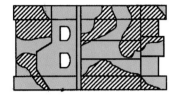

FRONT

REAR

Work from the elevations
first and then complete the
top of carrier.

SIDE

Issued by Cam. GHQ MEF.

Cam. Drawing No. A/194
Apr 43.

SCHEME FOR DISRUPTIVE PATTERNING.

HUMBER STAFF CAR.

SIDE

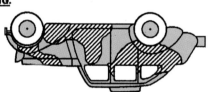

This design supercedes
G.O. 1650 of 1942.

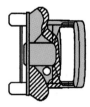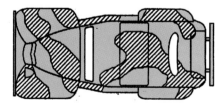

FRONT

REAR

Work from the elevations first
and then complete the top of
the car.

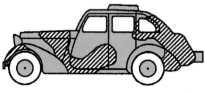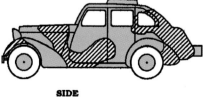

Issued by Cam. GHQ MEF.

SIDE

Cam. Drawing No. A/195
Apr 43.

SCHEME FOR DISRUPTIVE PATTERNING.   SIDE

10-ton FODEN.

This design
supercedes G.O.
1650 of 1942.

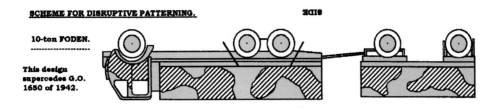

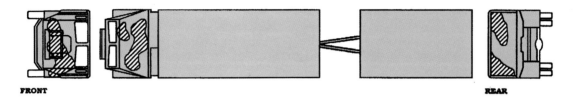

FRONT   REAR

Work from the
elevations first
and then complete
the top.

Issued by Cam. GHQ MEF.   SIDE   Cam. Drawing No. A/196
                                                                    Apr 43.

SCHEME FOR DISRUPTIVE PATTERNING.

25-pr GUN SHIELD.

This design supersedes
G.O. of 1942.

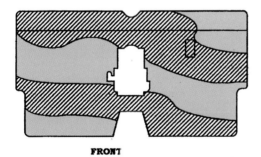

FRONT

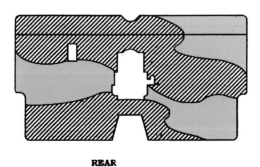

REAR

Issued by Cam. GHQ MEF.   Cam. Drawing No. A/ 197
                                              Apr 43.

The diagrams below have had the base colour of Light Mud added, with the shading representing the disruptive colour – Blue-Black (or Green). Note that some of the diagrams specify the use of White for counter-shading.

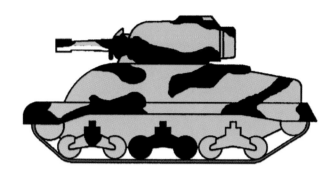

To illustrate the different 'look' that would result when different disruptors were used, these two illustrations have had the colours added; remember that the usual caution applies when trying to decipher a B&W image!

Again, the need for strict adherence to the patterns and of having a sharp edge to the colours was stressed. The order of priority for repainting was ordered to be:

- Vehicles in "Light Yellow" (ie those in a single desert base colour, most commonly Light Stone)
- Vehicles painted "Desert Pink" with or without "bright Dark Green" disruptive patterns.

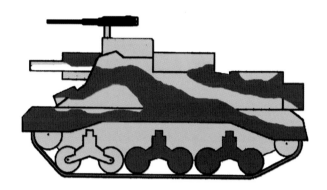

CORSTON of the Royal Wiltshire Yeomanry in scheme A/181.

Sherman coming ashore wearing pattern A/181. (TM 3456/B/3)

- Other schemes (which would include the 1st Army vehicles in MTP 46/4A schemes of G3 or SCC2, and those vehicles delivered directly from the USA and Canada in US Olive Drab).
- ACVs were not to be painted until ordered.
- Those vehicles painted in a base mixed from "5 parts Desert Pink to 1 part Dark Stone", with disruptive patterning in "dull Dark Green" and then not until ordered.

The formula mentioned here may well be the actual recipe for Light Mud, as in April 1943 the 5th Infantry Division in XIII Corps ordered 2000 Gallons of Dark Stone paint. Why would they order this out-of-use colour if they knew that a new colour was being introduced, unless in order to mix new paint to conform? The comments regarding two types of Dark Green are also interesting; it is open to debate what colours the author had in mind, but the "bright" colour might be No 7, the "dull" colour the darker No 6A. On 29th May 1943 HQ 8th Army complained that supplies of Light Mud and Blue/Black were "very limited, and in many cases nearest available colours will

Light Mud and a dark disruptor on this Sherman in Italy; note how much darker the base colour is compared to the Stone colours used in North Africa. (IWM NA6801)

Sherman Flail in Light Mud or Stone and Green, with the remnants of a roundel on the rear decks. (TM 2124/E/2)

A 5.5" gun in Italy, this time with a disruptive pattern on the upper surfaces over the base colour. (IWM NA5854)

This Humber Staff car in Italy in 1944 is still wearing a desert pattern of Dark Green over Light Stone. (IWM TR2149)

have to be used." This may indicate local mixing and/or use of similar (and maybe not so similar) colours off the shelf. The patterns however should still have been adhered to.[35] (In the papers of the National Federation of Association of Paint Colour & Varnish Manufacturers in the UK there is not, at any stage, mention of Light Mud, so it was almost certainly locally manufactured in the Middle East only. This would also strongly indicate the No 5 Grey and Light Mud were not the same colour.)

The use of White as countershading was continued in some of the patterns, including the lower third of barrels of tanks and inside the wheel arches of Jeeps and trucks. Vehicles with open bodies normally covered by tilts were to have the outside of the tilt painted in accordance with the pattern, but the inside might well have remained in any one of the many schemes previously used. Vehicles with open bodies not normally covered by tilts (e.g. carriers, SPGs and tank transporters) had the colours and pattern extended into the body. The order was clearly not able to be applied

to all vehicles in time for the invasions, as later instructions issued in Italy in the summer of 1944 refer to vehicles still in desert colours – see below.

However, not all vehicles photographed in action in Sicily conform to these or previous patterns, and there is an explanation for this. A suggestion was made on 16th April 1943 that rather than use these new Blue-Black disruptor based patterns in Sicily, vehicles being used for OPERATION HUSKY might be better painted with No 7 Green over either 11B Yellow Pink (ie Desert Pink) or No 5 Grey as this would be similar to the US vehicle camouflage scheme detailed in Operational Memorandum No 34 dated 9th March 1943. There is no confirmation whether this policy was ever adopted.[36] However, on 21st May 1943 AFHQ issued an order as follows:

– Vehicles engaged in operation HUSKY must be of a colour to suit the background of future operations.
– B class vehicles painted according to colours commonly used in UK - Dark Brown or Green sides and darkened roofs - will not need repainting, but all vehicles, partly or wholly painted in desert colours must be repainted according to annexed instructions.
– Certain 'A' class vehicles will be given a disruptive pattern as shown on the annexure.
– Painting will be carried out by units.
– Suitable paint is available through Ordnance channels.
– Two colours of paint are available, Light Stone and Slate Grey. If these paints are mixed in the proportions of not less than two parts and not more than three parts Light Stone to one part of Slate Grey, a special [light] grey is produced which is a suitable colour for the proposed painting.
– This type of paint is however not suitable for use on canvas.
– Therefore, insofar as the majority of 'B' class vehicles are equipped with canvas hoods, we are in a position to carry out the disruptive painting on certain 'A' class vehicles only.
– The colours in which all British vehicles, except those painted in desert colours, are now painted are themselves suitable to the background over which those vehicles are likely to operate. Disruptive painting is intended for dazzle purposes only (hindering accurate aim at vulnerable points), and is not likely to improve materially the chances of concealment.

The Annex issued with this order included four pattern examples, featuring very simple broad disruptive designs, and went into more detail:
– Designs should be varied slightly to avoid exact repetition, but the same scale and general disposition of painted and unpainted areas shown on the attached drawings must be preserved.
– a. Vehicles not painted in desert colours: The areas shaded should remain unpainted.
– The intention being to add areas of light grey which will be in contrast to the present dark grey [ie Light Mud], green or brown. Should the unpainted area contain more than one of the original colours, they must still remain unpainted.
– The following paint will be used: HA5555 Light stone mixed with HA6249 Slate Grey, in the proportion of not more than 3 parts and not less than 2 parts Light Stone to one part of Slate Grey.
– b. Vehicles already painted all over desert pink or yellow will be repainted with paint spraying HA5147 Khaki-Green on the shaded areas. The remaining surface will not be painted.
– c. Vehicles now pattern-painted desert colours and a darker colour will be repainted all over. Shaded areas Khaki-Green, remainder grey, mixed as described in a. above.
– All other vehicles at present wholly or partly painted in desert colours will be repainted in accordance with MTP 46 Part 4A in colours as follows:- Roofs and upturned surfaces standard camouflage colours 1A or 14 elsewhere Khaki-green No 3 or standard camouflage colours No 2 or No 7.

These instructions were accompanied by the following four drawings - it is not known if more were originally issued:

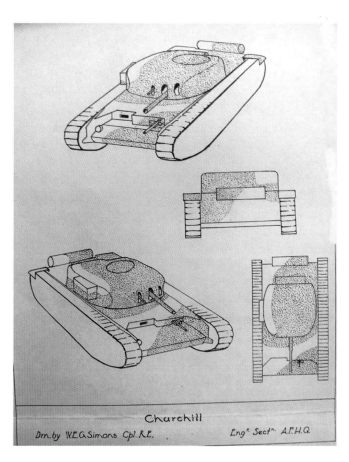

Charchill

Drn. by W.E.G. Simons Cpl. R.E.   Eng.ʳ Sect.ⁿ A.F.H.Q.

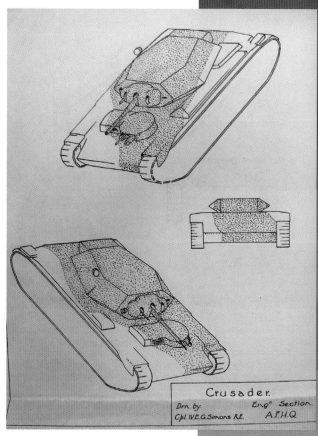

Crusader.

Drn. by   Eng.ʳ Section.
Cpl. W.E.G. Simons R.E.   A.F.H.Q

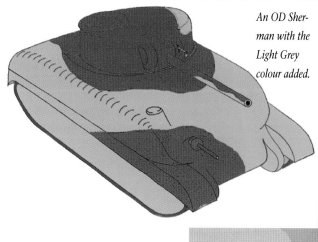

An OD Sherman with the Light Grey colour added.

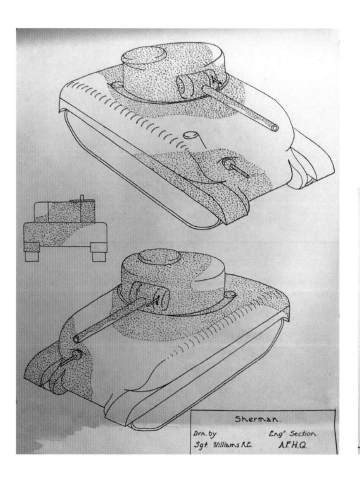

Sherman.

Drn. by   Eng.ʳ Section
Sgt. Williams R.E.   A.F.H.Q.

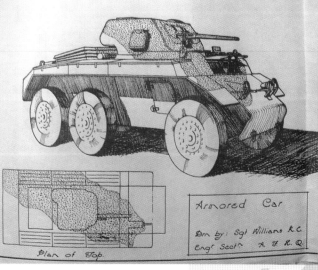

Armored Car

Drn. by: Sgt. Williams R.C.
Eng.ʳ Sect.ⁿ   A. F. R. Q.

Plan of Top.

The opportunity thus arose for some 'A' vehicles to be painted in a range of esoteric patterns. For instance, Light Mud and Blue-Black tanks, only very recently painted in that scheme, having large areas of the new Light Grey added over them. It is uncertain whether this order was carried out on a large scale, but as there were over six weeks from the order to the actual invasion, we must assume that many vehicles were painted in conformity to the order.[37] Indeed, many photographs of vehicles in Sicily and Italy from 1943 show evidence of the scheme being used, its low contrast making the colours difficult to decipher in B&W.

SICILY AND ITALY 1944 – 1945

By winter 1943 doubts were being raised at the effectiveness of these two schemes in Italy. On 4th November 1943 HQ 8th Army wrote to HQ 15th Army Group:

> Most EIGHTH ARMY vehicles are painted in the MEF disruptive pattern of light mud colour and black. It is becoming increasingly evident that this scheme is no longer effective camouflage, and formations have raised the question of its continuation…The simplest and most suitable scheme for all circumstances seems to be a uniform dark neutral green, similar to the Olive Drab paint used on American transport. (e.g. Service Green)

The letter concluded by asking for an early decision in order to allow paint to be demanded.[38] At the end of November a reply stated that whilst there was little evidence that the current scheme was ineffective, the Headquarters had no objection to the vehicles being repainted, as long as it was not solely done for uniformity. A suggestion was made that as there were no stocks of OD available in British stores, "Dark Green 6A or Dark Brown 1A or combination of both" was used. Having had this agreement, on 4th January 8th Army ordered quantities of "Olive Drab" paint, noting that deliveries were expected by spring 1944.[39] By April there were sufficient supplies of paint available to make this a reality although there were, as ever, many exceptions to the single-colour-only rule, including occasionally disruptive patterns applied over OD/SCC 15, and vehicles that remained in an out-of-date scheme. Priorities for repainting into OD/SCC15 were:
– Those vehicles still in a single desert colour – even in mid 1944!
– Those still in a desert base colour but with a disruptive pattern.
– Those in the 'original' 1943 Sicily/Italy scheme of Light Mud/Blue-Black.
– Those in MTP46 schemes of "Brown or G3 with a dark disruptive pattern or with horizontal surfaces Dark Brown or Black". This was to be done only when deterioration of the paint finish required the repainting of the vehicle, and not as a general rule.

War Office Camouflage Notes No 1 of December 1944 stated that "Allied Armies in Italy have recently adopted a policy of painting all vehicles in Olive Drab" – unfortunately the word recently is open to interpretation!

The practice of countershading barrels was also extended to the towed 6 Pdr and 17 Pdr Anti Tank guns, with an option to shade the upper third with Black, the lower third with White, both colours merging with the base Green along each side, although this seems to have been quite rare in practice. (I have also seen one film showing White undershading being used on a Churchill in Germany.) This policy was then extended to the 17 Pdr on the Sherman Firefly. A full debate on this subject were promulgated by a ME AFV Technical Letter of 26th January 1945, following a request in October 1944 for advice on how best to disguise Sherman Fireflies as normal 75mm gun tanks. Two methods were suggested; Method A being fitting a false muzzle brake half-way along the barrel (4'8" from the mantlet), with the underside portion of the barrel forward of this painted in 2½" White waves. Method B was the fitting of a dummy 75mm gun to the rear of the turret, traversing the turret 180[0] when out of action so that the 17 Pdr barrel was over the rear decks and the dummy gun pointed forward. Method A was to be used even when Method B was not. At least 24 tanks were fitted with the dummy barrels.

MISCELLANEOUS SCHEMES - ITALY

The British Army first used amphibious DUKWs in the Sicily and Italy campaigns, and at least some of these appear to have been camouflaged in a distinctive scheme of broad stripes in what seems to have been a shade of Brown over a base of one of the darker Stone colours, although of course this may have been Light Mud or the "special" Light Grey colour. The 51st Division DUKWs used in Sicily in 1943 certainly used this scheme, and it may have been more widespread than this. What is not clear is if this scheme was used only on DUKWs and/or only within 51st Division, or in some other combination of formation/vehicle type/period.

One rather famous variation to the Light Mud/Blue-Black scheme was used on Shermans by the Royal Scots Greys and some Indian tank regiments in Italy. It seems that neither unit used Blue-Black as the disruptor; the Scots Greys used a light Green (6A?), and the Indians a darker Green (7?). This may have been a deliberate variation to the specified colour, or in the case of the Indian unit the dark Green was possibly the original US Olive Drab that the vehicles were shipped in, the Light Mud 'base' having been applied over it. These units seem to have felt that the overall impact of the scheme was too light, and solved this by daubing a pattern of spots and splodges (probably Blue-Black SCC14 for the Scots Greys and Green SCC7 for the Indians) onto the Light Mud areas.

The Royal Scots Greys spotted scheme.

The Royal Scots Greys spotted scheme in Italy on Sherman SHEIK of A Sqn. (IWM NA7457)

EUROPE 1944 - 1945

In the spring of 1944, possible as early as January, the British Army began to procure stocks of a paint described as being 'similar' to US Olive Drab, and known officially as SCC No 15 Olive Drab. Three varieties of the British Olive Drab were produced, one for spraying, one for brush painting and later a third Bituminous version for canvas and tilts. Orders were issued in ACI 533 of 12th April 1944 that Olive Drab was to be adopted as the basic camouflage colour for all army equipment, in lieu of SCC2. The ACI did *not* authorise everyone to immediately reach for the paint brush; rather, as usual, it specified that painting was only to take place when due and necessary, and when all stocks of SCC2 had been exhausted. Paint supply, particularly early in its production run, was clearly still an issue. Bailey Bridges were an exception to this order; for safety reasons British components had to be left in SCC No 2 Brown to avoid mixing them up with US bridge parts, which were finished in US Olive Drab.

If SCC No 15 was not available, then a coat of either 'dark green' or 'dark brown' could be used. The latter probably means SCC No 2 although SCC 1A cannot be entirely ruled out[40], but the reference to the other Dark Green is less obvious. It is known that the British Olive Drab was a slightly greener shade than the US (hence the comment about it being 'similar' rather than identical) and therefore it is possible that it is BSC 7 or 24 being alluded to, but alternatively it could be SCC 7 or (less likely) SCC13. Many eyewitnesses recall their vehicles being 'dark green', and the terms 'Olive Green' and 'Khaki Drab' are also often used interchangeably.

Orders were also issued at the same time that 6 and 17 Pdr A/Tk guns *might* have the underneath of their barrels painted white, with the sides green and the topsides black. This followed the general thrust of the practice begun in North Africa on both tank and anti-tank guns, but seems to have been rarely done in practice - possibly because it was advisory, not compulsory. Sherman Firefly crews were extremely keen to avoid catching the eye of the enemy, as they would naturally

HRH Princess Elizabeth with non-patterned vehicles of a War Office training establishment, probably G3; note the L plate. (IWM TR2835)

become a priority target. In order to attempt to look like 'just any old short 75mm Sherman', they often painted the underside of the forward part of the 17 Pdr barrel with a wavy white line; sometimes the whole front portion was painted in one of these colours for the same reason, and sometimes cylinders representing false muzzle brakes were fitted half way along the barrel. It is not clear if the debate on the same subject in Italy noted above was as a result of policy coming from NW Europe, or vice versa.

Where US-produced vehicles were modified by the British - for instance the Sherman Firefly or the up-gunning of M10s with the 17 Pounder - patch-painting seems to have been the most common method of making good the modifications. As already noted, paint supplies were often scarce, and most instructions took pains to specify "paint only when necessary", and not just for conformity. Although SCC15 was not an exact match for US Olive Drab, it was probably accepted as close enough. This is not to say that some modified vehicles were not sprayed SCC15 overall, but it would seem reasonable to speculate that these were in a minority.

US Olive Drab, although not a British colour, is worth talking about in some detail, as tens of thousands of vehicles supplied by the USA under lend-lease were finished in this colour, including about 16,000 Shermans. The US Ordnance had been using a colour called 'Olive Drab' since before WW1. The colour was chosen as a compromise between the brown of the earth and the green of the foliage in temperate climates. It is therefore best described as a muddy dark Ochre - it was not Green. It was mixed using two pigments only - Black and Ochre. In 1920, the US Army named the standard formulation "Specification No 3-1 Olive Drab". It was this colour that remained the standard throughout WW2 for combat vehicles.

There were 3 finish variants: Gloss, Semi-Gloss and Flat (matt). The matt version does tend to look lighter in photographs, but this effect is caused by the finish, not the colour. In October 1940, the Quartermaster Corps, responsible for paint formulas and procurement, issued orders for all equipment produced from 1941 onwards to be in the matt version of Spec 3-1, which was now also confusingly called "QM Color No 22", but which was the same colour and finish nevertheless.

A Sherman of HQ 4th Armoured Brigade in September 1944 in US Olive Drab. (TM 2769/A/2)

To add interest - and even more confusion - the US Corps of Engineers issued their own colour chart, now calling it "Olive Drab Color No 9" - but again it was still the same colour! Whoever said watching paint dry was boring?

Another important ACI, 1100, was then issued on 12th August 1944, and which stated that as Olive Drab had now been adopted as the standard colour, "dark patterning on vehicles will be discontinued". A report later described why disruptive patterns were discontinued: "...partly because the introduction of recognition marks on vehicles rendered the continuance of disruptive patterning illogical...apart from this, however, experience had shown that against the air observer or air photographic interpreter, any normal field vehicle or equipment was too small to benefit by disruptive painting of any sort. Against the ground observer, in the case of static vehicles, disruptive patterns assumed some value, but only when vehicles were sighted (sic) against ideal backgrounds which suited the particular disruptive pattern." In short, the game was not worth the candle.[41] MTP 46/4A patterned vehicles, especially soft skins, were still to be seen throughout the rest of the war in Europe, as were some vehicles where the SCC2 had been over-painted with SCC15, leaving the original dark disruptive pattern undisturbed.

MISCELLANEOUS SCHEMES

Despite the ACI 1100 instructions not to use disruptive schemes, there was at least one British regiment (and probably more) that used Black disruptive patterns over Olive Drab on (at least some of) their tanks in 1944-45, and that was the 4th/7th Dragoon Guards in 8th Armoured Brigade - the often-used photograph of Sherman T152104 "Shaggy Dog" clearly shows this pattern in use. The method of the painting of the Black seems to indicate that it may have been applied only on the hull and turret sides and front, thus indicating its use as a local and possibly temporary scheme. The 8th Hussars may have also had some A30 Challengers in a two-tone scheme in early 1945. However, as vehicles were rendered unfit for service, the supply of replacement vehicles in standard paint schemes from delivery units would tend to 'dilute' the numbers of esoterically camouflaged vehicles remaining in units.[42]

SHAGGY DOG in a two-colour scheme. (TM 4811/B/6)

White snow camouflage paint, limewash or distemper may have been unofficially used by some units in Italy in the winter of 1943/1944, and the use of White sheets had been employed in training by the BEF in the winter of 1939/40[43]; but it was in North West Europe in January 1945 that the British Army issued, for the first time, official instructions on the use of snow camouflage for vehicles on operations. The 21ˢᵗ Army Group "Snow Camouflage Booklet", which also covered personal and positional camouflage, gave the following instructions for the camouflaging of vehicles:

```
Section 34. The use of Whitening Agents. In western Germany and in
the Low Countries snow conditions are seldom constant. Rapid thaws
may be expected and snow cover will not necessarily be continuous
over a wide area. Moreover, even in deep snow, buildings, woods and
other features still provide dark backgrounds. White paint or other
whitening agents should not, therefore, be used directly on vehi-
cles and weapons, but only as a means of whitening materials to be
put on them.
Section 35. White paint may be used, when practicable, on the under-
side of any tarpaulin which can be reversed ... and, as an alter-
native...to provide a temporary effective camouflage material, gar-
nished nets can be dragged in the snow.
Appendix.
Calico: supplied in rolls of three foot width. Suitable application,
making into patches with strings attached, to be used on artillery
or other nets, or for attachment to tank turrets, artillery and anti-
tank guns, reconnaissance vehicles and for general improvisation.
White Scrim: supplied in rolls of 100 yds length, three inches wide.
For garnishing nets, wire netting, helmet covers, wrapping of gun
barrels, small arms and for sniper aids.
```

Note that it was expressly forbidden to paint directly onto vehicles, in case of sudden thaws. This was widely ignored. On the hulls and turrets the lime- or whitewash was roughly applied, often missing out the areas immediately around vehicle markings, and often the rears of vehicles were not painted at all. Snow camouflaged vehicles often did not have the suspensions painted either, as there was probably not enough whitewash to go around, and the suspensions and lower hulls

Churchill in incorrect but common snow camouflage, applied to vehicle. Notice that the B vehicles are not whitewashed. (TM 4675/A1)

A Sherman and Churchill in winter coats; the suspension of the Sherman has not been whitewashed. (IWM B13788)

would soon get covered in mud anyway. The 'whitening materials' listed in the booklet included a White limewash made from rock lime and/or slaked lime, and either salt or powdered glue could be employed to obtain a more permanent finish. Where limewash only was used, the coating was not very durable and wore off easily, so that after a few weeks very few traces remained.[44]

The nearest Churchill has had whitewash applied only to the turret and the hull sides; doubtless the whole front is also white. The leading tank has also painted the hull rear.

Light Grey painted BARVs, DUKWs, bulldozers and the like were used in Normandy by units who were only expected to operate on the beaches, and not go further inland. The actual Grey used could have been one of the Admiralty Pattern colours, possibly AP507C "Light Mediterranean Grey", or BSC Light Grey No 31. In the case of tracked vehicles, the suspension was mostly left in the original colour, only the upper works being repainted. Many of these vehicles were operated by the REME who, in a tradition that they continue to this day, painted large rectangles in the Corps colours of Blue over Yellow over Red on the sides of their vehicles. Similarly, the Royal Marine Armoured Support Groups operated Centaurs still painted in SCC2. (Their vehicles were subsequently handed over to X Battery RA who used them inland for a short while.) The Shermans operated by the RMASG almost certainly remained in the US Olive Drab in which

Sherman BARV in a Grey base colour.

91

they were supplied, albeit with the extraordinary azimuth markings around the turret tops in White.

Red Oxide (BSC 46) was used occasionally as a camouflage colour, but was actually intended for use as a water-resistant and therefore rust-inhibiting undercoat, and was used as such when preparing bare metal or repairing damaged components, especially after welding. The inside of the cargo compartments of some lorries were also 'red-leaded'. In some cases, areas thus painted were not then finished with the correct camouflage colour, leaving the Red-Brown paint visible when the canopy was removed. Some sources indicate that at least a few DUKWs in Normandy had the lower part of their hulls painted in this colour, a possibility that seems entirely feasible.[45] Buffaloes

A Mountbatten Pink screen on a restored Valentine DD. (TM 6361/F/3)

and Terrapins used by 79th Armoured Division in March 1945 may also have had their hulls camouflaged with large patches of Brown or Red Oxide and Black over the US Olive Drab base.[46]

The screens of DD tanks were in various shades of light Tan or Khaki, most ending up as a very light bleached shade. At least some of the screen material started life as a Royal Navy colour called "Mountbatten Pink"[47], which has been described as a sort of Lavender/Mauve/Grey, if that description is at all helpful! The RN actually used two variants of it, Dark and Light, and it was meant to be particularly effective at dawn and dusk, dawn of course being when the DD tanks would be employed. The screens were quite fragile, and were often patched and/or sealed along the frames with Black Bostik glue. Some had a sort of basic "Plimsoll line" marking on the upper part of the canvas sides or rear, consisting of a number (4 or 5) of horizontal Black lines, each about 12" long and about the same apart, one above the other, to show the amount of freeboard when afloat. Some had their LCT numbers also painted on in Black, usually at the very top where they could still be seen whilst swimming. One source has indicated that the rear of some of the screens used on D-Day by the 13/18th Hussars were painted with a Green and White chequerboard design; Green and White was specified in that Regiment's Op Order as representing "Come On", so it may be that certain lead tanks only were painted in this way – see also Volume 4.

THE FAR EAST 1941–1945

There was one colour that predominated in the Far East during the war years, and that was of course dark Green, originally the pre-war semi-gloss DBG or possibly G3. However, prior to this, India had adopted Battleship Grey as the standard colour for vehicles, as the pre-war pattern experiments had concluded that so many different colours and patterns were required for different parts of that vast country, that there could be no one standard disruptive scheme. After this decision, disruptive patterning was very rare.

But...Military Training Pamphlet 10 India 1941 somewhat surprisingly detailed that the Caunter Pattern, using the Egypt Command colours of Light Stone, Silver Grey and Slate was to be adopted for training purposes in India. It also noted that: "For various reasons it has been decided to adopt the same scheme for training purposes in India although it is realised that the scheme may not be suited to certain types of Indian terrain. Should modifications to the colours and designs be necessary for operational purposes then instructions will be issued by Army Headquarters." It could be that the reason behind this seemingly bizarre order was that the precarious situation in the Middle East may have led to the staff considering transferring tanks from India to that theatre, and that this was actually sensible preparatory work.

A new Green colour generally called 'Jungle Green' coded as SCC 13 was introduced into use from early 1943 onwards, superseding the use of one of the other BSC/SCC Greens or locally produced colours used before that date. There are also indications that a new jungle colour was introduced in 1944 coded as SCC16 and called Dark Jungle Green or Very Dark Drab. War Office Camouflage Notes No 1 of December 1944 commented that:

> India have also adopted one colour only for all weapons and vehicles. This is Very Dark Drab No 207 in the SCAMIC (India) range. It is, as its name suggests, considerably darker than Olive Drab.

India probably means not only the sub-continent but also formations operating in other areas including Burma etc.

Therefore, vehicles in the Far East reported as being in "Dark Green" overall could be in DBG, G3, SCC 7, SCC 13, US Olive Drab, SCC16 or even SCC15! The best evidence is, as so often, the vehicle type and particularly the date.

VEHICLE SIGNS

The multitude of different signs that could be marked over these camouflage schemes will be the subject of detailed explanation in Volumes 3 and 4; Registration marks were covered in Volume 1. However, as a lead-in to those topics, it is worth realising the seriousness that the War Office attributed to the whole subject, by quoting from ACI 699 of 1940. This stated that "No titles or battery etc numbers are to be incorporated into any vehicle marking for the duration of the war". The message clearly was not received the first time round, as ACI 1085 of the same year had to re-emphasize: "All signs and markings not authorised WILL be removed from vehicles in the UK within 14 days". And were they? I'll let you be the judge of that…

RAF & RN VEHICLES IN WW2

Finally, a brief diversion away from the Army may be a useful way of wrapping up the WW2 period. When operating in the UK on airfields, where camouflage painting was less relevant, RAF vehicles tended to be painted BSC381C No 33 Blue-Grey. The RN used different shades of Grey, often BSC381C No 32 Admiralty Dark Battleship Grey or No 31 Light Battleship Grey.[48] These shades appear to have been used in matt and semi-gloss versions. In photographs of these vehicles the shades often appear very light in contrast to the darker shades on Army equipment. The Royal Marines, although part of the Royal Navy, usually followed Army schemes on their tactical vehicles.

As a general rule, when either RAF or RN vehicles were required to work in tactical areas, the prevailing Army scheme was used, although the letters RAF or RN as appropriate were often painted in White capitals on doors; the RAF also liked to paint small roundels on the fronts and/ or sides of their vehicles. RAF aircraft paints were almost certainly used by that service on some of its vehicles, with Dark Earth and Dark Green (or "sand and spinach" as it was informally called) being the most common in Europe, whilst Middle Stone and Dark Earth were used in North Africa. From about August 1941 though, adherence to Army colours and patterns seems to have become the norm.

ANNEX A – CHRONOLOGY

TABLE 1 – CHRONOLOGY OF WW2 MAIN COLOURS AND SCHEMES.

	NW EUROPE	Standard Patterns?	MEDITERRANEAN	Standard Patterns?
Pre-War	Deep Bronze Green.	No	Egypt - Pale Cream with Red Oxide disruptor.	No
1939	Feb 39 - Matt Khaki Green G3 is new standard base colour. Jun 39 - MTP 20 Schemes 1 (G3/G4) and 2 (G3/G5).	No	Jul 39 Egypt - Middle Stone and Dark Sand.	No
1940	Nov 40 - MTP46/4A schemes. Green G3 or Brown SCC2 base, with Dark Brown SCC1A as disruptor. (Dark Tarmac also used as disruptor from an unknown date in 1941)	No	Nov 40 Egypt - Caunter scheme in Light Stone, Silver Grey and Slate (or G3).	Yes
1941	Nov 41 – Brown SCC2 or Green G3 as base colour, with SCC1A as dark disruptor		Dec 41 Egypt/Libya - Light Stone or Portland Stone with one unspecified dark disruptor (usually Green or Black)	No
1942	May 42 – Brown SCC2 is new standard base colour.	No	Oct 42 Egypt/Libya - Desert Pink with Dark Green disruptor. (Alternatives Black, Dark Brown or Slate) Nov 42 Tunisia - 1st Army in NWE schemes.	Yes No
1943	Oct 43 - SCC14 Blue/Black to be disruptive colour.	No	Apr 43 - Light Mud with SCC14 Blue/Black disruptor or "Special" Light Grey bands	Yes
1944	Apr 44 - SCC15 Olive Drab base colour. Aug 44 – no disruptive patterns	No	Jan-Apr 44 Italy - as for NWE	No

ANNEX B – PAINT DETAILS

TABLE 2 - BSC 381C COLOURS FOR READY MIXED PAINTS

Colour	Also Known As Or Described As	BSC Reference Number	Remarks
Light Green G5	Light Green Medium Grass Green Light Bronze Green Olive Green	22	In use pre-war in various trials and units, and 1939-41 as disruptive colour in MTP 20 Scheme 2. R/G/B value 107/99/63
Khaki Green G3	Khaki Green Service Green New Service Colour (1939) Australian Std Colour J Nobel's KR5413 Ref 21-11 HA5638 HA5147	23	In use 1938-43. Announced in ACI 96 Feb 1939. Standard base colour in MTP20 Scheme 1 and 2 until 1942 when replaced by MTP46/SCC2. Possibly used in ME as darkest colour in Caunter Scheme. Similar to Middle Bronze Green but possibly a little browner – Khaki is a definite brown hue. It is unconfirmed therefore that G3 and No 23 are the exact same colour R/G/B value 83/81/69 (No 23)

Colour	Also Known As Or Described As	BSC Reference Number	Remarks
Dark Green G4	Deep Bronze Green Dark Green Service Paint (1939)	24	Normal base colour in semi-gloss until 1939. Matt variety in use 1939-41 as MTP20 Scheme 1 disruptive colour (mainly on Matildas). R/G/B value 73/73/67
Silver Grey	Light Yellow-Green Light Grey-Green	28	In use in ME in Caunter Scheme as disruptive colour. Faded to a slightly more blue shade R/G/B value 202/205/162
Light Battleship Grey	RN Grey	31	RN Colour Used on DUKWs, BARVs etc?
Blue Grey	RAF Blue RAF Blue Grey	33	Introduced in 1933. In use 1936-41 on RAF vehicles; still in use after then on airfields. Semi-Gloss finish. R/G/B value 70/76/85
Slate	Dark Slate Desert Grey Slate Grey Medium to Dark Grey with slight Blue tint HA6249	34	In use 1940-42 as dark disruptive colour in ME over BSC 61 or 64. Used as darkest colour in Caunter Scheme. R/G/B value 109/106/101
Terracotta	Deep Red-Orange	44	Infrequent use in ME 1938-1943 as disruptive colour. R/G/B value 151/81/79
Red Oxide	Red-Brown Red Lead	46	In use pre-war as disruptive colour (over BSC 52 base) by 11th Hussars and 6RTC. R/G/B value 115/68/66
Light Purple Brown		49	In use in 1940 as darkest (only?) colour in Caunter Scheme in Sudan. R/G/B value 92/65/69
Pale Cream		52	In use pre-war in Egypt as base colour (sometimes with BSC 46 over) by 11th Hussars and 6RTC. Stocks probably used up until exhausted. Interior of ambulances R/G/B value 238/197/150
Light Stone	Desert Yellow Light Yellow Sand ME Std Colour No 23 Australian Std Colour N HA5555	61	In use in ME 1938-42 as most common base colour. Signal 4/105 of Oct 41 specified BSC 61 as only base colour to be used. R/G/B value 202/153/103
Middle Stone	Hot Yellow	62	In use in ME 1938-42. More Yellow than LS. ME GO 370 of Jul 39 authorised use as base colour with Dark Sand as disruptive colour. Also used by RAF. R/G/B value 182/128/91
Dark Stone	Dark Yellow-Brown	63	In use in 1943 as base colour in Tunisia (XIII Corps). More Yellow-Brown than LS. R/G/B value 170/118/60
Portland Stone	Pale Cream with slight Green tint Birch Grey ME Std Colour No 11	64	In use in ME 1940-41 as alternative base colour to Light Stone. Used in Caunter Scheme. R/G/B value 213/187/164

Note: The R/G/B index allows an exact match using different colour systems.

R/G/B values based on modern mixes, and supplied courtesy of Cromadex

Australian Standard Colours are shown as approximations.

TABLE 3 - BSC 987c Standard Camouflage Colours 1942

Note: Although dated 1942, many paints in the chart were actually in service as early as 1939. Updated versions were issued dated 1944 and 1945. In Use dates are approximate, as schemes could be noted in use both before and especially after their official periods.

Colour	Also Known As or Described As	SCC Number	Remarks
Brown		1	Exact shade not known, but unlikely to be dark otherwise 1A would not have been required to be introduced.
Very Dark Brown	Plain Chocolate Very Rich Deep Brown Brown Dark	1A	Introduced in November 1940 at the insistence of the War Department. In use 1941-44 as dark disruptive colour in MTP 20 and MTP 46 patterns. Used in ME as dark disruptive colour. In use 1941-44 on tilts (ACI 1559). Possible use in 1944 as alternative to SCC15, Canadians only?
Brown	Service Brown Service Drab	2	In use 1941-44 as base tone. (Disruptive colours used over SCC2 were SCC14, SCC1A, SCC 4 or BSC 23.) ACI 2202 Nov 41 authorised use to restore faded tilts. Specification changed Dec 42.
Brown		3	Exact shade not known.
Earth Brown	Dark Earth Cup of Tea Australian Std Colour W Fawn	4	Possible occasional and unofficial use in 1942-44 as base colour (with SCC2 or 1A as disruptive colour.) NOT the same as RAF Dark Earth.
Brown	Medium Brown	4A	Introduced in December 1940, and probably only used by the Air Ministry
Grey	Light Grey Australian Std Colour G	5	No known army use
Green		6	Exact shade not known.
Dark Green		6A	Only one reference found to this colour, suggesting it as alternative dark disruptor to Blue/Black over Light Mud
Olive Green	Dark Green Dark Olive Green PFI Green Medium	7	In use 1941-44 on tilts (ACI 1559). Used as dark disruptive colour in ME, Sicily and Italy over BSC 61, SCC11B or SCC5. PFI denotes Phenol Formaldehyde Industrial, a paint polymer.
Mid Green		8	A green colour; no known application
Light Green		9	A green colour; no known application
Dark Brick Red		10	Appears on chart, no use confirmed.
Rust Red		11	Appears on chart, no use confirmed.
Terracotta	Deep Red-Orange Brick Red Tile Red	11A	Appears on chart, no use confirmed - possibly a slightly different shade to BSC 44

Colour	Also Known As or Described As	SCC Number	Remarks
Desert Pink	Desert Pink ZI Pale Brick Very Pale Brick Rose Pink Light Stone with a hint of Pink Very Pale Pink Yellow Pink	11B	In use ME 1942-43 on own, or as base in disruptive schemes on tanks. GO1650 of Oct 42 specifies use as base colour. (ZI stands for the Zinc content in the paint) Despite the apparent allocation of a BS987C code, there is no mention of this colour being manufactured in UK, so it may have been mixed in North Africa only.
Very Dark Grey-Green		12	Appears on chart, no use confirmed. Described as Grey in 1940 dated notes.
Jungle Green	Dark Green	13	Appears on Chart dated 1939, but probably not used on vehicles until introduced into use Far East 1943-45.
Black	Blue-Black Charcoal	14	In use 1941-44 as dark disruptive colour in ME, Italy and NW Europe. Described as a "gritty" colour, probably meaning rough pigments were used with a noticeable effect on the painted surface.
Olive Drab (Amendment 1 to chart Dec 1944)	Olive Green Khaki Drab Australian Std Colour M	15	In use 1944-45. Authorised by ACI 533 Apr 44 as standard overall colour in Europe. More green than US Olive Drab. ACI 1100 Aug 44 authorised use to dye tilts.
Very Dark Drab (Amendment 2 to chart Jul 1945)	Dark Jungle Green AKA SCAMIC 207	16	Introduced at some point in 1944 as an alternative to SCC No 13. Few references exist, but possibly very similar to Deep Bronze Green.

Notes: Colours would often be in use well before the official amendment was promulgated.

PFU indicated that the paint was Prepared For Use, meaning no water or other dilutant was required. Alternatively, in paint chemistry, it can also stand for Phenol Formaldehyde Urea.

TABLE 4 – SCC DESCRIPTIONS

The following colour descriptions of BS 987C Standard Camouflage Colours were included as Annex A to MTP 46 Part 3 Huts Camps and Installations. The descriptions - and the cautions shown in brackets - make interesting reading, and whilst it must be remembered that these refer to the use of these colours on other types of paint for static installations only, the colours were standardised and therefore the descriptions are consistent with those used on vehicles:

Number	Description	Number	Description
1	Brown	8	Mid Green (dangerous)
1A	Very Dark Brown	9	Light Green (very dangerous)
2	Cup of Coffee and Milk	10	Useful dull Red
3	Cup of Tea	11	Rusty Red
4	Cup of Weak Tea	11A	Bungalow Tiles Red
5	Very Light Grey	11B	Sandy Pink
6	Dark Green	12	Clean Cold Grey
6A	Very Dark Green	13	Dirty Grey
7	A useful Warm Green	14	Black

TABLE 5 - NON-STANDARD COLOURS

Colour	Also Known As Or Described As	Remarks
US Olive Drab	Lusterless Olive Drab Specification 3-1 Olive Drab No9 QM Color No22	More brown than UK Olive Drab. In use on Lend-Lease supplied US vehicles.
Nobel's Dark Tarmac	Dirty Dark Grey Faded Black Paint Spraying No 4 HA5149	Not coded. Pre-war experimental colour. ACI 1559 of Aug 41 authorised continued use as dark disruptive colour over G3.
Dark Sand	Light Brown with Reddish tint	Not coded. Pre-war experimental colour. Used in ME 1936-1939. ME GO 370 of Jul 39 authorised use as dark disruptive colour over BSC 62.
Light Mud	Light Khaki Light Mud Brown Mud Grey Dark Sand Dirty Beige Grey	In use 1943-44 in Sicily and Italy as base colour; rarely used on its own. (GO dated Apr 43.) This shade appears to have been personally selected by General Dempsey when commanding XIII Corps, and was apparently mixed locally in Egypt and Tunisia - there is no mention of this colour being manufactured in UK, so it was probably mixed locally only.
Snow White	White Paint PFU Arctic CS700	Available but not officially authorised as snow camouflage

MISCELLANEOUS

In1944 the following paints were in use with the supply codes shown (the HA numbers):

PAINT PREPARED FOR USE (PFU)

HA0209	Black GS
HA0218	Blue GS
HA0225	Brown, Khaki Colour
HA0231	Buff GS
HA0241	No 15 Olive Drab Stoving
HA0243	No 15 Olive Drab Heat Resistant
HA0244	No 15 Olive Drab
HA0255	Green GS
HA0275	Red, Bright GS
HA0279	Red Oxide of Iron
HA0282	Service Colour GS [Note: This is probably Khaki Green G3]
HA0293	White Lead GS
HA0186	Red Lead Dry
HA0296	Yellow Amn [Note: Presumably means ammunition]
HA5912	No 15 Olive Drab Petrol Resistant

PAINT SPRAYING

HA0242	No 15 Olive Drab
HA5199	Black Flat
HA5149	Dark Tarmac No4
HA5715	No 2 Brown Anti-Gas

BITUMINOUS EMULSION

HA6145	No 15 Olive Drab
HA6188	No 1A Brown Dark
HA6194	No 2 Buff
HA6179	No 7 Green Medium
HA6180	No 11A Brick Red
HA6184	No 14 Black

WOOL GREASE EMULSION

HA6221	No 1A Brown Dark
HA6222	No 2 Buff
HA6228	No 7 Green Medium
HA6233	No 11A Brick Red
HA6237	No 14 Black

PIGMENTED BALLOON VARNISH

HA6339	Shadow Black
HA6340	Dull Drab
HA6341	Putty

The names are as given, and may represent paint listed in either BSC 381C and/or BSC 987C systems. Describing No 2 as Buff (rather than Brown) is almost certainly an error or a poor choice of words.[49] The special type of cellulose paint called Pigmented Balloon Varnish (PBV) was available to use on rubber devices and those made of "balloon fabric"; this was issued in three colours as noted above. It is not known if any of these were ever pressed into service as camouflage paints, but as they were designed to be used (among other applications) on the inflatable dummy vehicles used for deception, there is a chance that this might have happened occasionally...[50]

Additional paint colours other than camouflage shades were also in use, often for sign-writing purposes, including BSC 381C No 1 Sky Blue, No 5 Oxford Blue, No 6 Royal Blue, No 14 Golden Brown, No 31 Light Grey, No 37 Signal Red, No 38 Post Office Red, No 56 Golden Yellow and No 57 Orange; as well as Black, White and Aluminium/Silver; most in both matt and gloss varieties. Local paints were often used, particularly in the Middle East. The Admiralty and the RAF had their own paints, charts and designations.[51]

Finally, for those interested, an ACI in early 1945 even listed how paint cans were to be marked! From August 1944 the standard official scheme was that they were to be Black overall, with one or two bands at the very top in the same colour as that inside (Black paint was identified by two narrow White bands). Spray paint was shown by a one 3" wide band, and brushing paint by two 1 1/2" bands. Marked on the bands showed other details, including the code for the paint, eg HA0279.

ENDNOTES

1 NA File TSIR 246/125

2 Courtesy Cromadex. It must be realised that computer monitors do NOT give true results for colours, and that some colours may have changed slightly over the years; they should be used with caution therefore. Because of the problems of accurate reproduction, sample colours or swatches have NOT been included here.

3 NA File TSIR 246/125

4 That at least two different printers produced their own versions of the colour cards is important, as this could tend to allow more deviations from the true reference color, especially under wartime printing conditions.

5 NA File DSIR 4/2423

6 Forward Control Vehicle was, by then, an almost archaic term relating to the driver's position where there was no true bonnet, whereas a Normal (or Bonneted) Control Vehicle had a bonnet. It did NOT refer to Forward Air Controllers.

7 From 1942 the old designation of 'RASC vehicles' was dropped, all non A or C vehicles being labeled as B vehicles. (See Volume 1)

8 As always, the exceptions - Matilda I and II were both white inside.

9 Canopies always fade in different ways; even today uniformity of colour is very difficult to achieve.

10 In fact it was never amended but was replaced, finally being cancelled by an ACI in late 1941.

11 For the researcher it also acts as a fairly foolproof method of differentiating between MTP20 patterns and the similar looking MTP 46/4A Foliage pattern.

12 It is interesting to note that MTP 46 Parts 4, 5 and 7 were not officially cancelled and replaced until November 1957!

13 ACI 1160 of May 1942 added that Nobel's Dark Tarmac No 4 could be used as the dark disruptive colour if 1A was unavailable.

14 NA File WO 195/1895

15 Ibid

16 Moorhead African Trilogy p 21

17 General Orders were issued by Commands; they were numbered and dated, with new numbers starting again from GO 1 each January 1st. Therefore, both number and date need to be established.

18 The word "regular" was subsequently amended to "Irregular" by ME GO 575 of 24th October 1939.

19 This GO cancelled GOs 40 and 648 of 1937, and GO 13 of 1938, which therefore must have also covered the subject of camouflage.

20 That familiar term, Western Desert, was a British definition specifically meaning the Egyptian desert, as opposed to the Sinai (or Eastern) Desert.

21 My emphasis.

22 Order issued by Brigadier Shaw, see also endnote 16; courtesy of Mark Mackenzie and AWM.

23 Delaforce Taming The Panzers p 43 Olive Green clearly just means one of the many Greens rather than a specific named colour.

24 Delaforce Taming the Panzers p 42.

25 HQ BF in P & TJ memo CR/PAL/17390/7/G of 14 Aug 41.

26 NA File WO 201

27 Birch Grey refers to Portland Stone, again illustrating the minefield of paint names!

28 Zinc Iodide, a paint pigment.

29 Though not all; a number of photographs show 40RTR training in UK in Light Stone painted Valentines, prior to embarkation.

30 Moorhead African Trilogy p 32

31 Types used included Vickers Light VIC, Matilda, Valentine, and A9.

32 Other IWM images are GM 328 and GM 474

33 Horne, Monty: The Lonely Leader, p 54. Also noted in other sources, including Robin Neillands' Eighth Army.

34 It is not known why the previous patterns were not simply re-used with the new colours; in any case, the old patterns and colours were officially discontinued from April 23rd.

35 NA File WO 204/2964

36 Ibid

37 NA File WO 204/4814

38 NA File WO 204/4769

39 NA File WO 204/2964

40 The 4th Canadian Armoured Division Provisional Operational Standing Orders of 11 June 1944, Section 21 Camouflage, stated: 2 (a) 'A' vehs: One colour only will be used which may be any of the following: SCC Number 1A (dark brown), SCC Number 7 (dark green), Olive Drab (dark green).

41 SCRDE Project No 686 June 1970.

42 In June 1945 the RAC held nearly 32,000 AFVs, and had lost nearly 18,000. See Forty Handbook p 69.

43 A Mk IV Tank photographed in February 1918 appears to have been whitewashed – see IWM Q 56824

44 I have used these types of whitewashes in BAOR in the 1980s, and they often had a distinctly Yellow cast to them, although this may have been due to an over-long storage time.

45 The painting is "Arromanches D-Day +20", by Barnett Freedman, who was in Normandy at that time.

46 82 Assault Sqn RE

47 AKA Plymouth Pink.

48 R/G/B values are 96/113/105 and 182/199/186 respectively.

49 NA File WO 204/7964

50 NA File WO 287/210

51 RN paint specifications (known as Rate Book Patterns) required their paints, for fire safety reasons, to be supplied as separate 'pastes', only to be mixed when required on board ship, and then in very specific ratios. Who is to say that some of these pastes could have been used by the army in extremis and that in those instances the ratio control was not as specified? NA File TSIR 246/125

Infantry Tank A11 or Matilda I as used by the BEF in 1940. GLENLYON was a 7RTR tank. (as shown by the initial letter G), and the White square was a BEF recognition sign. She is painted in MTP20 Scheme 1 of G3 and G4 Greens.

Another A11 in MTP20 Scheme 1, this time Vickers-built DEMON of 4RTR – again, the initial letter of the name showing the RTR naming convention. The AOS number 4 with White bar above indicated the unit – details will be in Vol 3.

A pilot model of the Humber Scout Car, marked as P2. The scheme shown here,
Mickey Mouse using Slate or Nobel's Dark Tarmac over SCC2 is hypothetical, as MM
was only rarely applied to armoured vehicles.

An early Sherman II of 1st Troop C Squadron
10th Hussars at El Alamein October 1942. 10th
Hussars were the junior regiment in the 2nd
armoured Brigade, after the Bays and the 9th
Lancers.

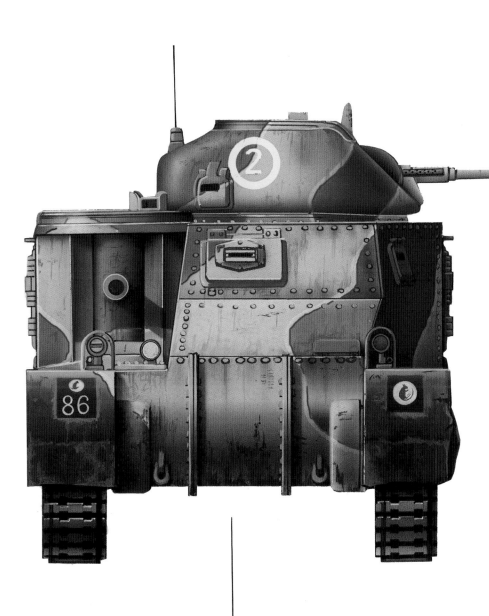

An M3 Grant of 7th Armoured Brigade in North Africa mid-1942. This vehicle is from C Sqn the Sherwood Rangers Yeomanry, the second senior regiment in the senior Brigade. She retains a 22nd Armoured Brigade scheme, showing she has been handed over between units at some point.

An Archer 17 Pounder self-propelled gun of the 43rd Wessex Division in Holland, late 1944. the vehicle is in overall SCC15, and the markings identify it as belonging to the Divisional Anti-Tank regiment RA, the 59th. E1 indicates the first gun of the 1st Troop, 3rd Battery.

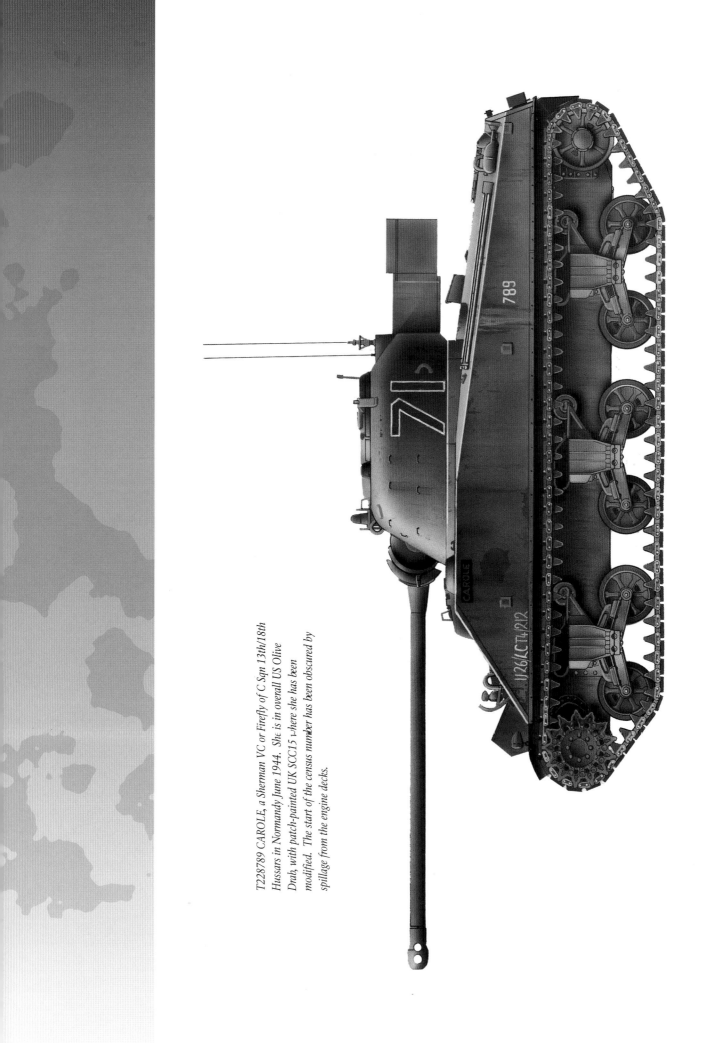

T228789 CAROLE, a Sherman VC or Firefly of C Sqn 13th/18th Hussars in Normandy June 1944. She is in overall US Olive Drab, with patch-painted UK SCC15 where she has been modified. The start of the census number has been obscured by spillage from the engine decks.

SUB-UNIT MARKINGS AND CALLSIGN SYSTEMS

INTRODUCTION

This chapter will investigate the various methods that have been used to differentiate between both sub-units and individual vehicles on the battlefield. For obvious reasons it would be impractical to attempt to use the registration mark system for this purpose - although vehicle names have occasionally been used for this purpose, as discussed in Volume 4. What was needed was a method using symbols and/or letters and/or numbers, placed in a prominent position, large enough to be seen from a distance, and coded in such a way they could not be easily deciphered by the enemy. The two main components of this chapter will deal with these methods: Sub-Unit Markings and Callsign Systems.

TERMINOLOGY

Sub-unit Markings are those which allow a sub-unit (be it Squadron, Company, Battery etc.) to be identified easily from the others in the unit; generally such systems used symbols. WD publications often referred to these as "tactical signs", although confusingly this terminology was sometimes used in other contexts.

Callsign Systems are a combination of letters and/or numbers which allow individual vehicle (and sometimes also the sub-unit) identities to be established. These subjects are closely linked, and therefore each will be discussed separately but where appropriate together, within chronological periods. The term CALLSIGN only came into use because of the advent of military radio communications. Each vehicle with a radio was then in effect a station on the radio net. For reasons of both security and brevity, a system of identifying oneself and referring to each station was required. Using letters and/or numbers this system became known as Callsigns. It was logical therefore to display the same callsign used on the radio nets on the outside of the vehicle in order to identify it clearly to friendly forces. Sometimes the term "Turret Number" was also used in this context. For convenience and clarity, all such letter/number systems, even those predating radio, will be referred to herein as Callsigns, even though this is of course not strictly accurate.

RN Car probably in late 1914 with the plain RN designation. (TM 637/E/2)

WORLD WAR ONE – ROYAL NAVY

The Royal Navy Air Service Armoured Car Batteries developed the earliest system of tactical identification marks which in effect served as their callsigns. From 1914 their cars and armoured lorries were marked with the legend R.N. in large White letters on the sides and rears (O.H.M.S. was used on the fronts), and later, around mid 1915, the abbreviation R.N.A.S. in 12" high letters in White, Red, Black or Dark Blue was painted on the vehicles. Large 3' high

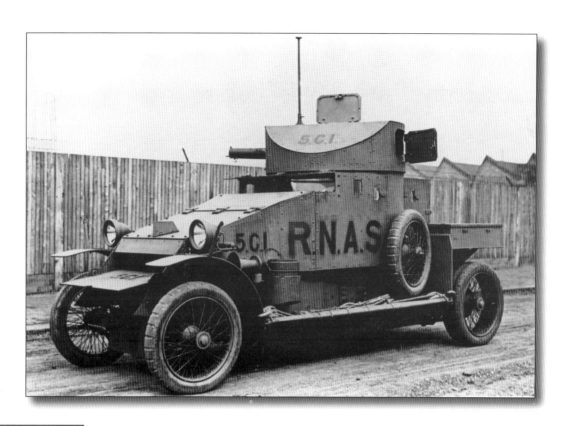

Lanchester 5.C.1. (TM 532/A2)

R.N.
R.N.A.S.
R.N.A.S.
R.N.A.S.
R.N.A.S.

White numbers were sometimes used on the lorry sides to differentiate between vehicles, the size clearly indicating that recognition from a distance was a requirement. Examples include 68 and 71.

By 1915 the RNAS Armoured Car Division had grown to 8 Squadrons (later 15), each of 3 Sections, and a more elaborate (though hardly secure) system came into use. An alpha-numeric system was chosen, with the Squadron number first, then the Section letter (A, B or C), and finally the individual vehicle number, all separated by full stops; for example 14 Squadron B Section 4th vehicle was marked **14.B.4.** These markings were positioned on the bonnets, on the angled turret flaps and sometimes on the rear in characters 6 - 12" high, they were generally painted in the same colour as the R.N.A.S. marking, which continued to be used.

Seabrook Lorry 5.C.5. (TM 532/A3)

TANKS

The Heavy Section (later Branch) Machine Gun Corps also quickly realised that there was a need to identify both Companies and individual vehicles (but not for some reason the level in-between, Sections), and used an alpha-numeric system of the Company letter followed by the individual Company tank number, for example C.19 was tank number 19 in C Company. The intention at the early stage was merely to allow the tanks to identify each other on the battlefield. The tanks deployed in Gaza did not use this system.

At first these markings were painted in White or Yellow in a small (c3") font on the front horns and the nose, with the prefix letter often being a little larger than the numbers, but it soon became

A6 unusually had its identifier painted on the sponson. (TM 86/C/3)

B56, with the vision slits camouflaged. (see Volume 1). (TM 1557/C/1)

C24. (TM 86/A/1)

J18. (IWM Q 9248)

clear that these could not be seen from a distance, particularly when covered in mud, so the size was subsequently increased, although the dimensions, colours and positioning varied hugely between different units and at different times. The specified dimensions in July 1917 were 18 inch characters with a 2 inch width, often in either White or Red outlined with White, although smaller versions were used, and some units still preferred large letters with smaller numbers. The basic system however remained constant throughout the war – a Company/Battalion prefix letter followed by a 1 or 2 digit number.

The need to identify vehicles both from the rear and also from the air later became apparent, so the system was again refined. Tanks started to show their callsign on the rear of the tank for the benefit of the infantry (and also staff observers watching the progress of an attack from the rear), and on the roof to allow the same for aerial observers. The basic alpha-numeric system remained unchanged, even when the Companies grew into Battalions. One exception may have been F Bn, who were reported to have used 6 instead of F in spring 1918; two records refer to tanks **6/11** and **6/36**. As before, styles and positions varied between units or formations.[1]

In addition to their normal callsign, Wire Cutter tanks at Cambrai carried the additional letters **WC** in dark letters on a White background on the rear fuel tank as a means of identifying their role to the following infantry. Tanks converted to supply usually had their sponsons blanked off and the legend **SUPPLY** painted across them in 12" White characters; on one example, probably the 10th Battalion, the word **BAGGAGE** was used instead; the difference possibly being Supply meaning combat supplies, ammunition, fuel, rations etc, whereas Baggage represented personal equipment and accommodation stores. F Battalion at Cambrai used the letters **FS** to denote their supply tanks, G Battalion used **GS** at Ypres, and not all supply tanks were marked at all. Wireless tanks were often marked with **WT**, or, in the case of F Battalion, **FW**.[2] Mk IX Infantry Carrier Tanks used 24" high letters **IC** with a two digit number (e.g. **IC 15**), but as none of these saw action this may well have been a post-war system.

A Wire Cutter tank. (IWM Q 6413)

Supply tanks in action. (IWM CO 3250)

A Whippet with the callsign 9. (possibly the tank of Lt Sewell VC 3rd Bn Tank Corps). (IWM STT 229)

There were a couple of exceptions to the general rules. When the Medium A Whippet tank was introduced in 1918 the Battalions operating it dropped the alpha-numeric system and used either letters or numbers. In some cases the letter represented the initial letter of the tank commander's surname, for example A277 CLARA commanded by Sgt Parrot used a P – what happened in the case of duplication is not recorded.

Gun Carrier Tanks in 1918 used the letters GC followed by a 3 digit number, and this seems to have been used both for the original purpose as the vehicle census number (See Volume 1) and also the means of identifying the vehicle tactically, although their names may also have been used for this purpose.

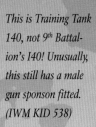

Gun Carrier Tank GC141 being used as a Supply vehicle. (TM 1567/A/1)

This is Training Tank 140, not 9th Battalion's I40! Unusually, this still has a male gun sponson fitted. (IWM KID 538)

Training tanks (often easily identifiable by blanked-off sponsons) used in both France and England used large one, two or three digit White numbers on the front horns and nose to identify individual machines. The range of these bears no obvious relationship to the numbers of tanks produced or to their census numbers, so an element of deception could well be at work by allocating random numbers to make the fleet look larger. Examples noted include: 7, 20, 68, 74, 106, 200, 282, 415, 450 and 815. (Care must be taken not to confuse the I prefix of 9th Battalion with the figure 1.)

When the 17th Battalion Tank Corps was equipped with Austin armoured cars in 1918 some of the cars had a light-coloured rectangle painted onto the angled plate above the rear mudguard; possibly Yellow, Light Blue or even White, and with a slightly larger version on the radiator cover

A.277 P CLARA

A277 CLARA was commanded by Sgt Parrott, hence the P marking.

102

Training Tank 102 - NOT an 'I' Bn tank - with "shadowed" numbers.

Training Tank No 140 from the right side, marked on the front horns and the nose. (TM 1549/C/4)

plate at the front. A type of callsign was painted onto both these plates. One photograph shows a large dark (c18") figure 3 on the front, with a much smaller (c6") figure 2 inside the curve of the 3. This probably indicates 3 Company No 2 Section, or possibly No 3 Section No 2 car, in which case it would be likely that different coloured backgrounds would have been used to differentiate between the Companies. Other cars though simply bore a single Company letter.

3₂

This 17th Bn Austin bears the callsign 22 - B Company No 2 Section? (TM 882/E/2)

SYMBOLS

During the war the French had devised a graphically-based system for differentiating between sub-units, using playing card symbols, and some Battalions of the Tank Corps experimented with this, including the 6th and 8th Battalions. The colour of the symbols denoted the sub-unit; A Coy used Red, B Coy Blue, and C Coy Green. The symbol denoted the section: the first section used Hearts, the second Diamonds, the third Clubs, and the fourth Spades. Each individual tank within the section was then represented by one of the cards of that suit. A diagram issued by 8th Battalion showed the position of these devices on a Mk V to be just forward and above the grill on the rear horns.

Disabled Female 2732 with the Ace of Spades on the sponson, therefore it is the first tank in the fourth section – the company cannot be identified without knowing the colour of the symbol. (TM 5040/C/5)

F4 with the Four of Hearts in Red. (IWM Q 7278)

BETWEEN THE WARS CALLSIGNS

Various systems were used in the inter-war period. In the UK, the 5th Battalion continued to use the WW1 system through the 1920s until the late 1930s; for example E24. The other battalions appear to have dropped the system at some point in the 1920s. Some tanks were not marked at all, but many others bore either two or three digit numbers, without prefix letters, much as training tanks had done previously. Where markings were used, they were generally on the rear of the hull sides and the hull rears on medium tanks, in 18" White characters. The turret sides were sometimes marked as well. It should be remembered that this was a period of experimentation, and piecing together the sequence of the systems applied to different Battalions at different dates is still incomplete; this applies to both individual callsigns and the related sub-unit geometric designs detailed below.

Abroad, it seems that individual units adopted whatever system suited them, probably because no official instructions on the subject existed, so there were no orders to be disobeyed! In Palestine, the 1920 Pattern Rolls-Royce armoured cars of No2 Armoured Car Company were marked with section letters and then individual car numbers, in black characters on either side of the bonnet and on the angled turret flaps; for example C.3. In India in 1935, the 2nd Light Tank Company RTC used section letters, known ones were T, I and N. The choice of these letters was related to the use of signal flags, as described in Volume 4.

As a general rule though, not only in the inter-war period but also well into WW2, only those vehicles fitted with a radio were likely to bear an individual marking; those without radios were often only identifiable at Section or Platoon level.

Medium II E17 of 5th Battalion RTC. (TM 55/G/6)

N and I Sections of 2nd light tank company RTC together. (TM 6122/F/1)

THE DEVELOPMENT OF GEOMETRIC MARKINGS

In instances where armoured vehicles were used in large numbers together, it was clearly necessary to be able to differentiate quickly and accurately both between similar regiments and also the squadrons or companies within those regiments. From 1927 onwards many different systems were trialled in the EMF/EAF manoeuvres on Salisbury Plain, and one of the first recorded systems was detailed in the War Office publication *Tank Training Manual Volume 1*, issued in 1930, although the markings contained therein had been seen in use as early as 1928. This system shown below and modified subsequently was the forerunner of the geometric system still in use. The basic premise was that a clearly identifiable shape should be used to represent each sub-unit, sometimes allied to a numerical system that identified the troop/section or even individual vehicle.

It will be seen straight away that this method could lend itself to confusion, as identifying the second from the third Sections at any distance must have been difficult. This system almost certainly failed in the field, as the RTC subsequently carried out more experiments to identify an improved version.

Other instructions contained in the 1930 publication including specifying a particular identifier for radio-equipped tanks, mimicking WW1 practice; tanks with wireless were still few and far between. These were to have a White square or rectangle painted on their sides bearing the letters RT, presumably in Black. Vehicles belonging not to the companies, but to Battalion HQ and to the transport echelon, were to have a regimental flag device painted on them. The 1930 publication Armoured Car Training used a very similar system to the one above, but as there were only independent Armoured Car Companies at that stage, not Regiments, only the A Company circles were required.

APPENDIX I

DISTINGUISHING MARKS

1. Signs when used will be as follows :

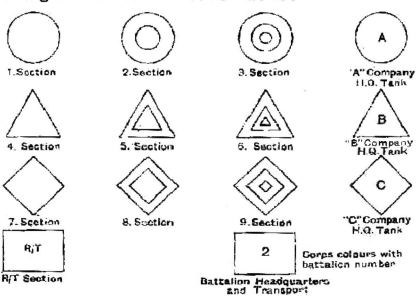

2. In the case of medium tanks the diameter of the outside circle and each side of the oblong or square will be 10 inches, and of the triangle 12 inches. The lines will be white, ½-inch thick.

Medium I with B Coy No 5 Section markings and callsign 51. (TM 254/F/1)

Armoured Car Company symbols 1930.

APPENDIX I
DISTINGUISHING MARKS

1. Signs when used will be as follows :—

1 Section

2 Section

3 Section

Coy. Comdr's Car

2. The diameter of the outside circle will be **10 inches**. The lines will be white, ½ inch thick. The number in the circle on the company commander's car will be the number of the company.

Signs will be painted both in front and rear. The position will be standard throughout the company.

3. The commander of every unit will fly a small flag from his car. The shape will be as follows :—

Section >   Company 5 <

Colours will be :—

1 Sec. ...	...	...	...	Red
2 Sec. ...	...	...	...	Yellow
3 Sec. ...	...	...	...	Green

The company commander's flag will be in R.T.C. colours with the company number in black in the centre.

By 1934, the width of the White lines for company signs had been doubled to 1", and the designs themselves had also changed, to make them visible over longer distances. A simpler system of using horizontal or vertical lines within the symbols to indicate the sections was in use, with the following structure being employed:

THE 1934 SYSTEM	Company HQ	1st Section	2nd Section	3rd Section
A or First Coy Sections 1-3	Ⓐ	○	⦶	⊖
B or Second Coy Sections 4-6	△Ⓑ	△	△	△
C or Third Coy Sections 7-9	◇Ⓒ	◇	◇	◇

Also by 1934, each RTC Battalion CO used a numbered RTC pennant exclusively to indicate their command vehicle, and this was painted on each side of the turret (with the point facing to the rear).

Another series of geometric shapes were noted in use with a battalion of the RTC in 1937, all of which were painted in White in broad (c1") lines. This was similar to the 1934 version but the filling in of either parts of or the entire symbol was an attempt to reduce the risk of confusion, and to increase identification ranges:

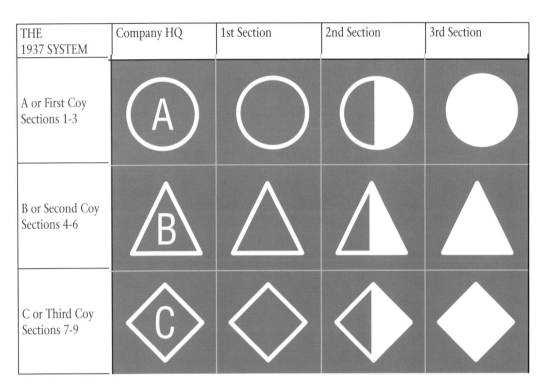

THE 1937 SYSTEM	Company HQ	1st Section	2nd Section	3rd Section
A or First Coy Sections 1-3				
B or Second Coy Sections 4-6				
C or Third Coy Sections 7-9				

Other symbols noted in photographs but not identified as belonging to a particular system were:

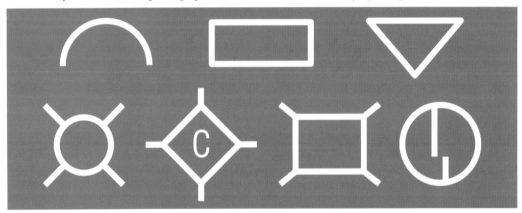

The use of symbols based on the letter D was also quite prevalent. They were seen depicted exactly as the letter would be written, but were sometimes used as mirror-images, or laid down (both ways); as they were lying on their sides, the latter two versions came to be known as the 'Lazy D'.

Medium II tank T145 with an upside-down triangle device. (TM 879/D/3)

WORLD WAR TWO

GEOMETRIC SQUADRON/COMPANY MARKINGS

By 1939 the different geometric systems trialled before the war had been rationalised and a standard system established. So it was that the familiar geometric system was laid down as the war started and which has lasted, with some minor amendments, to the present day. The exact sizes of the symbols were specified. The symbols had been changed around again, probably in an attempt to make the symbol more akin to the letter – a triangle was most similar to a letter A, a circle best represented the letter C, and so B Sqn got the square! The overall dimensions were to be 9" on small and light vehicles; in other words picture an invisible square of that size with the appropriate symbol painted neatly inside it. For medium tanks and Matilda IIs the size was increased to 18".

From April 1940 the presence of a fourth (D Coy/Sqn/Bty) sub-unit was catered for by the adoption of a solid vertical bar symbol, and from 9th March 1944 a sixth symbol was made available to allow Infantry Battalions to denote an extra (Support) company.[3] This was similar to the D Coy symbol, but placed horizontally. In some cases, including in the BEF in 1940, these symbols were painted as blocks, rather than outlines. Motorcycles were too small to make a symbol useful, so were meant to have the extremities of the front and rear mudguards painted in a band of the Sqn colour – Red for A, Yellow for B, and Blue for C.

SQN/COY/BTY	SYMBOL
A or First	△
B or Second	□
C or Third	○
D or Fourth (where used) Added in April 1940	▯
Support Company Added in March 1944	▭
HQ (and RHQ) In many cases an elongated, rather than equilateral, diamond was used.	◇ ◇

Daimler Armoured Car with A Sqn 3 Tp sign.

An A30 Challenger with the B Sqn sign and Troop number 3 on the turret rear. (IWM B 11051)

Below: 3RTR A13 in Calais 1940, from SHQ B Sqn.

*Spot the marking!
Note the B squadron
square on the trunk-
ing, probably placed
there because the full
height trunk would
have obscured the
turret markings.*

An RHQ Light Mk VI from an unidentified regiment in France – and in trouble! Note the squashed shape of the diamond.

GREENOCK of C Sqn 7RTR in 1st Army Tank Brigade. This Brigade in mid 1940 consisted of 4, 7 and 8RTR, and was the only one to have used this unusual hatched design of squadron marking. This symbol appears to have White or Yellow hatching on a Black in-fill.

Another related standardised system had also come into use at the same time, in which the seniority of each regiment within its parent formation[4] governed the *colour* that the regiment used for its geometric markings.[5] Within formations, strict seniority order was insisted upon, so the senior regiment was to paint its tactical markings in Red, the next senior used Yellow, whilst the junior regiment was to use Blue.[6] On those rare occasions where a fourth unit of the same type was present within the formation, Green was to be used. Un-brigaded units (and this generally included Reconnaissance and Armoured Car regiments, as well as the Army Tank Brigades whose units were

The A Sqn marking. It appears that the colour of the geometric shape represented the regiment within the brigade. (Red, Yellow and Blue) - in this case then this is Blue for 8RTR. The presence of diagonal lines within the shape may represent a Section/Troop leader, and the colour of those lines the troop number. (See also the explanation of commander's pennants in Volume 4). (IWM H2425)

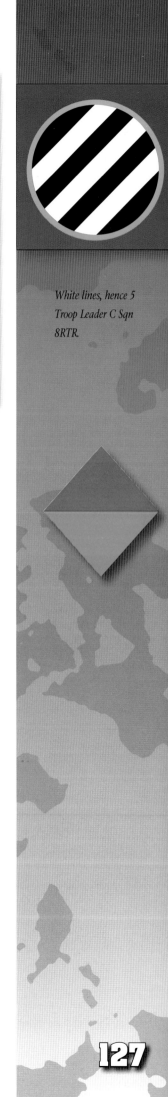

White lines, hence 5 Troop Leader C Sqn 8RTR.

parceled out to different formations on a temporary basis) were meant to use White. It can be seen then that regimental seniority was of crucial importance, as it would determine both the Sqn/Coy insignia colour and also the Arm of Service colour/number (See Volume 3). A few regiments may have chosen to use the colour/seniority system *within* the unit, so that A Sqn used a Red triangle, B Sqn a Yellow square etc, but it is difficult to identify which units did this and when; it was not common. A 7RTR RHQ Matilda named GREYNA in 1940 used the diamond, but painted it as a block Red over Green, their battalion colours, rather than the correct colour; it may be this was used to denote the Commanding Officer.

As an example of both the effects of changing formations and of non-conformity, 5RTR in the Western Desert in January 1941 started by using Purple (probably BS No 49) tactical signs, when part of 3rd Armoured Brigade in 2nd Armoured Division. (Why did they use a non-standard colour? We do not know, although they appear to have also used the colour in France in 1940.) The size of the signs was noted in the very detailed instructions issued by the Battalion Technical Officer, also giving the colour to be used. It was ordered that lines were to be 1¼" thick, and dimensions were to be:

– HQ Diamond – 18" high, each side 12" long
– A Sqn Triangle – 16" base, 14" high
– B Sqn Square – 14" sides
– C Sqn Circle – 9" diameter
– D Sqn Vertical Bar – 18" high

From June that year the regiment changed to Yellow signs whilst in 4th Armoured Brigade in 7th Armoured Division, and then changed to Blue in July 1941 when 8th Hussars and 3RTR joined. From the very detailed instructions issued, it appears that these changes were not only implemented quickly but were also considered to be routine.[7]

In fact, many units did not change formation very often, and a significant number remained with their original formation throughout the whole of the war, but there was still a considerable amount of inter-formation movement, which should automatically have generated a large amount of re-painting. However, whilst the formation and AOS signs generally *were* repainted in short order – not to do so would have caused confusion – it is less certain that Sqn/Coy insignia would have been done either as quickly or indeed at all. For one thing, many units as a matter of course deliberately disregarded the colour/seniority rules and used either White because it stood out well, or a dark colour because it would NOT stand out well, or even a colour related to the regiment's

history. 3RTR used their regimental colour of Green during Operation Crusader in 1941, rather than the Yellow that they should have employed.[8] Some units even used 'shadow' effects, outlining (for instance) White or Yellow signs with Red shading to give a 3-D effect; an example of this was the 9th Lancers at Alamein. And in a few cases, generally involving 'B' vehicles, the symbol could be 'blocked', or filled-in, rather than just outlined, possibly because no callsign or troop number was required inside the symbol due to the vehicle type.

Sizes could and did vary between formations, and even within units, although instructions for standard sizes were often issued. The publication *Middle East Training Pamphlet No 2 Part V Army Tank Brigade Operational Standing Orders*, dated December 1941, detailed in Annex J the various markings to be used. The sizes of the geometric signs (known in the publication as "Tactical Signs"), were as follows:

– HQ Diamond – 16" high, each side 12" long
– A Sqn Triangle – 9" sides
– B Sqn Square – 12" sides
– C Sqn Circle – 12" diameter

All lines were to be 1½" wide. Interestingly, rather than ordering the use of White, as was the accepted procedure for Army Tank Regiments operating Infantry Tanks, the instruction was given to paint the symbols in "Red Yellow Blue as allotted to Tank Battalions".

In the Western Desert, where vehicles on arrival had their European scheme over-painted with one of the desert schemes, there was a fairly common tendency not to paint the new base colour within the sign, so that the inside remained in the old darker base colour, often G3 or SCC2. It could be that this was done deliberately in order to make the symbol and callsign within stand out more, and it was also easier for the paint teams. Similar instances also occurred in the European theatres, including that recorded in Terence Cuneo's painting "Scots Guards in Bocage 1944", which shows three Churchills of that regiment with A Squadron triangles in White with Red infills.

Shermans of the 9ᵗʰ Lancers in 1942 with shadowed symbols and troop numbers. (TM 2716/D/5)

A 1ˢᵗ Armoured division Jeep in May 1942, with a 'blocked' diamond symbol. (IWM E11507)

In some cases the symbols and colours could be allocated to smaller units than regiments. 7th Armoured Division issued specific instructions on 22nd November 1941 allocating symbols to the two RE Field Squadrons under command. 1 Fd Sqn were to use Red, 7 Fd Sqn Yellow. In both cases, the Sqn HQ was to use the HQ diamond, while each Tp would use the appropriate Sqn symbol: 1 Tp the triangle, 2 Tp the square etc. Individual vehicle numbers were to be painted inside or alongside the symbol.[9]

Valentine PENELOPE of 8 Tp B Sqn 40RTR with an in-filled symbol. (TM 5054/C/2)

This Churchill called FELTHAM pictured in October 1943 has an in-filled A Sqn symbol, with the Troop number in White. (IWM H33372)

THE 'STANDARD' INDIVIDUAL CALLSIGN SYSTEMS

Signals publications of the war period do not explicitly list callsigns to be used, almost as if the need for a secure and adaptable structure was not recognised. This gave formations and units wide scope to develop their own systems. Where instructions were issued, they tended to deal with the application of markings, rather than the underlying system.

Most often in the early years just the troop number was displayed on vehicles, the troop leader himself being identified by a pennant, and sometimes vehicle names were used as well (see Volume 4). In August 1939 MTP 22 stated that "Troop etc. numbers" were to be painted in White <u>beside</u> the Sqn/Coy symbol; however, from December 1940 the order was amended in that the numbers were to be painted in the same colour as the symbol, and could be either inside <u>or</u> beside the symbol. In the publication Middle East Training Pamphlet No 2 Part V Army Tank Brigade Operational Standing Orders, dated December 1941, Troop Leaders in Infantry Tank regiments were instructed to mark their troop number inside the sign in White, whereas the remainder of the tanks in that troop were to use the same colour as the geometric sign (see below). In some cases in UK mid-war the Sqn symbol had a dot inside it, with the troop number outside, so the dot might well have been used to show the troop leader's tank. In North West Europe, 29th Armoured Brigade vehicles all used Yellow numbers, whatever the colour of the geometric sign.

The 'standard' callsign system adopted later in the war by the RAC for tanks was very simple and flexible. It was able to be adapted for different establishments, so whether the Regiment had three or four Squadrons, or each Squadron had up to five Troops, the basic system could be used. In essence, each troop was numbered individually and consecutively through the regiment; the Troop Leader used this number, his Troop Sergeant used the suffix A; the Troop Corporal B; and if a fourth vehicle was present, it would use C. Squadron Headquarters vehicles would use the letters HQ inside their respective geometric sign, and Regimental Headquarters would use the letters RHQ inside a diamond. So in a three-squadron, four-troop regiment, the troops would be numbered 1-12; three examples are shown:

Churchill IV GRAIL of A Sqn, with a dark infill and troop number 5 inside the symbol. (TM 1779/A/4)

Shermans in Tunisia; note that the troop number 4 has been marked in two different styles and in such a way as to blend into the camouflage scheme, particularly on the second tank. (IWM NA 1574)

A Sqn 2nd Troop Sergeant	B Sqn 3rd Troop (7 Tp) Leader	C Sqn 1st Troop (9 Tp) 2nd Corporal
2A (triangle)	7 (square)	9C (circle)

It should be stressed that the number of troops drives this system – a change of establishment that created an additional troop for each squadron would cause a lot of repainting! A variation of this system avoided this issue by referring to each troop in squadron terms; thus the third troop in B Sqn were simply called 3rd Tp B Sqn. The geometric symbol was still used as the method of differentiating between squadrons. So the same examples would look like this:

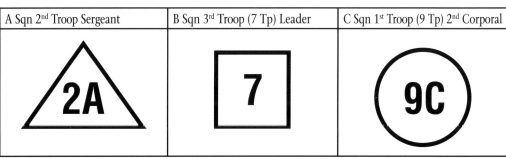

A Sqn 2nd Troop Sergeant	B Sqn 3rd Troop Leader	C Sqn 1st Troop 2nd Corporal
2A (triangle)	3 (square)	1C (circle)

Sherman 3A of B Sqn. (IWM NA 23754)

Normandy, July 1944 – Sherman Firefly 3C of B Sqn; note that the symbol on the nose merely gives the troop number. (3), whereas the rear of the turret provides the actual callsign. (IWM B7743)

3RTR A10 in Greece 1941; this is the Troop Leader 12 Tp C Sqn – 3RTR used small A and B suffixes for the two NCO tanks in each troop during this campaign.

Another variation was used by 1RTR on their Cromwells and Fireflies in Normandy in 1944. The three SHQ tanks were numbered 1-3, 4 was not allocated or was used as a spare, and the four troops in each squadron used 5 – 8 inclusive, with suffixes as before; again, the geometric symbol differentiated the squadrons. The same examples now look like this:

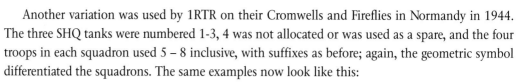

A Sqn 2nd Troop Sergeant	B Sqn 3rd Troop Leader	C Sqn 1st Troop 2nd Corporal (Firefly)
6A	7	5C

The fighting squadrons in 1RTR in 1944 therefore looked like this:

1RTR (1944)

A, B and C Sqns (Cromwell plus 1 Firefly per Tp as 4th tank)

1 – OC	2 – Sqn 2IC	3 – SSM	
5	5A	5B	5C– 1 Tp (Tp Ldr, Tp Sgt, Tp Cpl 1, Tp Firefly)
6	6A	6B	6C– 2 Tp
7	7A	7B	7C– 3 Tp
8	8A	8B	8C– 4 Tp

A Light Stone Valentine of 40RTR training in UK in late 1941; it displays a very large B Sqn symbol with the troop number 6 inside. (TM 1789/C/1)

COLOURS, SIZES AND POSITIONS

The sizes of the symbols varied considerably. In those cases where the callsign was painted inside the geometric sign, its size was limited by the space available. In 1940, most geometric signs were quite small. By 1941 the fashion was for very large signs, often as high as the turret sides would allow, and callsign characters could also be much larger as a result. By 1944, the geometric signs had been reduced in size once more.

NON-STANDARD (TWO-DIGIT) CALLSIGN SYSTEMS

It could be that different views on the visibility of the callsign led to the non-standard systems that developed. Where the callsigns were painted in a small font, one of the 'standard' systems could be used, as it would be difficult for the enemy to read it from a distance. Those units that required better visibility (ie the ability to see who was who at greater ranges) may also have had concerns that the various leaders at Regiment, Squadron and Troop level were too easily identifiable by the enemy using the standard system, and thus developed their own regimental two-digit systems. This would account for the fact that none of the two-digit systems noted in use seemed to have been the same!

In these two-digit systems, each tank was given a unique number, often, although not always, in a numerical sequence relating to seniority. A similar system had been developed by the RTC between the wars, being used in UK on Medium tanks and in Egypt on Light tanks. 32nd Army Tank Brigade at Tobruk appear to have used very large (c12-18" high) one or two digit numbers (without sub-unit signs) on vehicle sides in either Yellow or White.

A Matilda II at Tobruk in December 1941 with a large 2 on both turret and hull. (IWM E6920)

Users of the two-digit system generally painted their numbers in very large characters on the turret sides, with slightly smaller versions on the turret rear. (Hull sides were infrequently used as well.) Colours varied; for example:

Another Matilda II in North Africa with a large single digit call-sign. (AWM 023716)

- Yellow outlined with White (Sherwood Rangers Yeomanry, 144th Regt RAC)
- Red outlined with White (13/18th Hussars)
- Blue outlined with White (East Riding Yeomanry)
- The vehicle base colour outlined with White (4/7th Dragoon Guards)

Three examples of the two-digit system are:

13/18ᵗʰ Hussars (D-Day)

RHQ (Sherman)
10 – CO   11 – 2IC   12 – Int Offr 13- RHQ Tank

A Sqn (Sherman DD)
21 – OC   22 – 2IC   23 – SHQ Tank
24, 25, 26, 27 – 1 Tp (Tp Ldr, Tp Sgt, Tp Cpl 1, Tp Cpl 2)
28, 29, 30, 31 – 2 Tp
32, 33, 34, 35 – 3 Tp
36, 37, 38, 39 – 4 Tp

B Sqn (Sherman DD)
40 – OC   41 – 2IC   42 – SHQ Tank
43, 44, 45, 46 – 1 Tp
47, 48, 49, 50 – 2 Tp
51, 52, 53, 54 – 3 Tp
55, 56, 57, 58 – 4 Tp

C Sqn (Sherman; last tank in Sabre Tps is Firefly)
60 – OC   61 – 2IC   62, 63 – SHQ Tank
64, 65, 66, 67 – 1 Tp
68, 69, 70, 71 – 2 Tp
72, 73, 74, 75 – 3 Tp
76, 77, 78, 79 – 4 Tp

Opposite: 13/18th Hussars Sherman Firefly callsign 71 CAROLE. (TM 2995/F/2)

144th Regt RAC (1944)

Recce Tp (Stuart)   1-11
AA Tp (Crusader)   12-17
Spare   18-19
RHQ (Sherman)   20-23
Spare   24-29
A Sqn (Sherman)   30-49
B Sqn (Sherman)   50-69
C Sqn (Sherman)   70-89

Note that RHQ 144 RAC wisely concealed itself inside the overall scheme, so as not to appear too senior - pity the poor Recce Troop leader!

Opposite: Sherman of RHQ. The 'unlucky' number 13 was sometimes avoided both for troop numbers and callsigns; the 13/18th Hussars, maybe because of their pre-amalgamation history, were evidently not superstitious! (TM 4701/D/2)

1st Northamptonshire Yeomanry (1944)

RHQ not known, possibly 20, 21

A Sqn (Sherman)
17 – OC   18 – 2IC   19 – SHQ Tank
1, 2, 3, 4 – 1 Tp (Tp Ldr, Tp Sgt, Tp Cpl 1, Tp Cpl Firefly)
5, 6, 7, 8 – 2 Tp
9, 10, 11, 12 – 3 Tp
13, 14, 15, 16 – 4 Tp

B Sqn (Sherman)
22 – OC   23 – 2IC   24 – SHQ Tank
25, 26, 27, 28 – 1 Tp
29, 30, 31, 32 – 2 Tp
33, 34, 35, 36 – 3 Tp
37, 38, 39, 40 – 4 Tp

C Sqn (Sherman)
SHQ not known, possibly either 41 and 42, or 59, 60 and 61
43, 44, 45, 46 – 1 Tp
47, 48, 49, 50 – 2 Tp
51, 52, 53, 54 – 3 Tp
55, 56, 57, 58 – 4 Tp

Units of the 79th Armoured Division used two systems which operated side by side. Armoured vehicles mostly used a two-digit system, as did Buffaloes. However, the RE specialist vehicles in the Assault Regiments carried additional markings on D-Day, which reflected the lane each grouping

Sherman 82, possibly Staffs Yeomanry. (IWM B 6904)

worked in on the Normandy beaches, rather than the callsign. The digit represented the lane number, and the suffix letter specified the role within the lane. For instance, 77 Assault Sqn RE used 0A for the Officer Commanding, and the layout for the vehicles in lane 4 was:

4A   AVRE with Carpet device

4B   AVRE with SBG

4C   AVRE with Bobbin

4D   AVRE with Plough

4E   AVRE with Plough

4G and 4H were allocated to Sherman Crabs from the supporting RAC regiment, but most RAC regiments did not seem to bother marking these lane codes on the vehicles, relying on their normal 2 digit callsign. The exact allocation of these lane codes would depend upon the nature of the obstacles identified in each particular beach and lane.

The Guards Armoured Division always used its own systems throughout the war. The first version involved letters (A, B, C and D etc) indicating the company headquarters tanks, with numbers being used for each troop/platoon; these were placed inside the company symbol, with no method of differentiating between the individual vehicles in the troop. The Guards tended to reverse the classification of Squadrons and troops; whereas a 'normal' unit would have (for example) B Sqn 2 Troop, the Guards might use Number 2 Sqn B Troop! Additionally, they preferred to paint such callsigns on all four sides of the hulls, rather than the more common turret locations. A second system noted in use in 1944-45 used turret numbers with letter suffixes, in which the troop leader bore the troop number alone, with A to C suffixes being used as described above.

Some of the two-digit callsigns seem to have been adopted in an ad-hoc manner in the field, and were applied in a very rough and ready way. The 11RTR Buffaloes used in the Rhine Crossing of March 1945 had White two-digit numbers painted in a sloppy freehand on their sides and rears, giving the impression that they were a last minute addition, although whether this was for security reasons is unclear.

Churchill AVRE callsign ?B at speed. (TM 2242/A/1)

1st Lothian & Border Horse Sherman Crab '75'. (TM 2121/D/4)

Cromwell BLENHEIM – the tank of OC No 2 Sqn 2nd Bn Welsh Guards in the early system. (TM 1800/E/1)

A Guards Covenanter belonging to the 2IC of No 3 Sqn. (TM 4733/B/6)

Guards Sherman Firefly 2C using the later system. (TM 4201/A/1)

Buffalo SEVENOAKS of 11RTR with a hastily applied two digit callsign. (TM 3061/A/5)

SOFTSKIN CALLSIGNS

The use of anything resembling callsigns on 'B' vehicles during WW2 was extremely unusual, and very few photographs exist of the practice; a Bedford lorry of an unidentified unit in 1944 was noted carrying a very large (the height of the side of the canvas canopy) figure '4', possibly in Red outlined in White, but this is a rare example and the reason for it is unclear.

In Normandy RASC DUKW units used a system of markings similar to callsigns. White or Yellow letters were stencilled on a Black rectangular background, centrally between the top two ribs on the side; this so as to be visible when the vehicle was in the water. There were 11 Companies of DUKWs used on D-Day, each of 3 Platoons of 24 vehicles, eight of which are listed below; the 'missing' three presumably used the same system.[10] The RASC Company number in clear was used followed by the Platoon letter, and then the individual vehicle number within the Platoon. The Platoon letter and vehicle number were often repeated on the front horizontal surface of the nose.

23/A1 to 23/A24, 23/B1 to 23/B24, and 23/C1 to 23/C24
27/A1 to 27/A24, 27/B1 to 27/B24, and 27/C1 to 27/C24
101/A1 to 101/A24, 101/B1 to 101/B24, and 101/C1 to 101/C24
199/A1 to 199/A24, 199/B1 to 199/B24, and 199/C1 to 199/C24[11]
237/A1 to 237/A24, 237/B1 to 237/B24, and 237/C1 to 237/C24
297/A1 to 297/A24, 297/B1 to 297/B24, and 297/C1 to 297/C24
377/A1 to 377/A24, 377/B1 to 377/B24, and 377/C1 to 377/C24
633/A1 to 633/A24, 633/B1 to 633/B24, and 633/C1 to 633/C24 [12]

DUKW number 19 of B Platoon, 633 Coy RASC. (IWM B5174)

THE ROYAL ARTILLERY SYSTEM

The Royal Artillery developed a completely unique system of designating types of Unit, Batteries, Troops and individual vehicles, originating in the 1930s. Some elements of the system still linger on today – for instance, Battery Captains are still known as the 'BK', because a K symbol was used to designate his vehicle. The signs used were originally up to 9" square, mimicking the Arm of Service marking; the basic colour of the signs was similar to the RA AOS marking – Red and Blue with White characters, but this system must not be confused with the Arm of Service system (see Volume 3). Both were used together; the AOS denoting the type and identity of the unit, the RA system identifying the Battery and vehicle/role.

RHQ vehicles used a horizontally halved Red over Blue sign identical to the RA AOS background plate. The Batteries had a ¾ Blue sign with one quarter painted in Red, the red quarter denoting the Battery. The senior Bty had a Red square in the top right quarter of the sign, the next senior Bty bottom right, then bottom left, and finally the 4th Bty (where formed) used the top left quarter. (Survey Regiments alone used Yellow instead of Blue for the Battery squares, and the RHQ sign of a Survey Regiment had a small Yellow triangle in the top right-hand corner. However, survey vehicles within a Field etc regiment did not use this system.)

The signs were carried front and rear, and occasionally on the sides or on cab doors. On guns

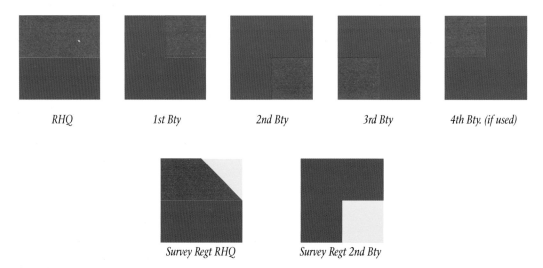

| RHQ | 1st Bty | 2nd Bty | 3rd Bty | 4th Bty. (if used) |

| Survey Regt RHQ | Survey Regt 2nd Bty |

with shields they were often painted onto the outside of the shield on the left-hand side, and on the rear left of limbers. Later these markings were often made much smaller, about 4" square, and were often mounted immediately above the AOS plate. Superimposed upon the signs in White was a system of letters and/or numbers denoting the role of each individual vehicle:

Common Regimental markings:		Common Regimental markings:	
CO	Z or Z1	Quartermaster	Q1
Regt 2IC	Z2	QM Stores Vehicles	Q2, 3, 4
Adjutant	A or A1	Cooks	Q5
RSM or Chief Clerk	A2	QM Water Bowser	Q6
RHQ Staff	A3	R Signals Officer	S1
Medical Officer	A4	R Signals Detachment	S2 - 7
Survey Officer	SUR 1	Motorcycles	MC1 – 7
Survey Parties	SUR 2, 3, 4	HQ Carrier/Scout	T

Common Battery markings:	
Battery Commander (BC)	X or X1 (used on Carrier Op or OP tank)
Battery Commander (BC)	X2 (used on runaround - jeep etc)
Battery Captain (BK)	K or K1
Battery Captain's Assistant	K2
Command Post Officer	Y1
Battery Survey	Y2
REME	(in LAA Bty only)

Common Battery markings:	
Signals	M1 – 5
B Echelon Ammunition	AMN1 – 6
BQMS	Q1
BQMS Stores Vehicles	Q2 – 4
BQMS Water Bowser	Q5
CP/Rear Link Signals	H
Motorcycles	MC1, 2, 3
BSM	J1

Field (Towed) Battery:

	1st Bty		2nd Bty		3rd Bty	
	A Tp	B Tp	C Tp	D Tp	E Tp	F Tp
Tp Cmdr (OP)	RA or R1	RB or R2	RC or R3	RD or R4	RE or R5	RF or R6
GPO	GA	GB	GC	GD	GE	GF
Tp Ldr	TLA	TLB	TLC	TLD	TLE	TLF
Tractor Limber & Gun 1	A	E	A	E	A	E
Tractor Limber & Gun 2	B	F	B	F	B	F
Tractor Limber & Gun 3	C	G	C	G	C	G
Tractor Limber & Gun 4	D	H	D	H	D	H
Spare Tractor	AB	EF	AB	EF	AB	EF
Spare Limber	CD	GH	CD	GH	CD	GH

Self-Propelled Battery:

	1st Bty		2nd Bty		3rd Bty	
	A Tp	B Tp	C Tp	D Tp	E Tp	F Tp
SP Gun 1	AA or A1	BA or B1	CA or C1	DA or D1	EA or E1	FA or F1
SP Gun 2	AB or A2	BB or B2	CB or C2	DB or D2	EB or E2	FB or F2
SP Gun 3	AC or A3	BC or B3	CC or C3	DC or D3	EC or E3	FC or F3
SP Gun 4	AD or A4	BD or B4	CD or C4	DD or D4	ED or E4	FD or F4

Medium (Towed) Battery:

	1st Bty		2nd Bty	
	A Tp	B Tp	C Tp	D Tp
Gun Tractor 1	AA	BA or BE	CA	DA or DE
Gun Tractor 2	AB	BB or BF	CB	DB or DF
Gun Tractor 3	AC	BC or BG	CC	DC or DG
Gun Tractor 4	AD	BD or BH	CD	DD or DH

Some parts of this system were standard across all types of RA unit and were detailed in Artillery Training Pamphlet No 2A; others were particular to a unit's role. It must be realised that the system was modified in various ways, in various units, and at different times; the examples above show a fairly 'standard' system, but gives common alternatives where these are known.[13] Where the tables refer to 1st Battery, 2nd Battery etc, this is a purely numerical way of expressing relative precedence, as the batteries in the regiment will have been known by their actual title, often one of the historical RHA or RA names, such as "Bull's Troop", "The Residency" or "The Battleaxe Company". For example, the RHA regiments listed their batteries within regiments as follows (please don't ask why!):

1RHA – A, B, E.

2RHA – H, I, L.

3RHA – D, J, M.

4RHA – C, F, DD.

5RHA – G, K, CC.

6RHA – C, D, F.

11RHA – A, B, E.

13 RHA – G, H, I.

Disabled Sherman on the BC of K Bty 5RHA in August 1944; is that White paint on the rear of the turret roof? (IWM B 9093)

The 'runabout' truck of a Battery Captain. (IWM B6325)

A Quad in trouble in Italy; it has a large C1 on the side, presumably C Tp 1st Gun. (IWM NA 7669)

Similar roles sometimes used the same letter, the distinction being made by the type of backing plate or by suffixes; thus Q1 on a Regimental sign denoted the QM, whereas Q1 on a Battery sign denoted the BQMS. These characters could either be marked 4" high centrally within the sign, or could use 2-3" characters in the blue portion of the quarters; this latter system originating with AA units and eventually becoming the norm. (Note that these codes were NOT used as the Callsigns on radio nets.)

3rd Bty BQMS. (1st style)

4th Bty BQMS. (2nd style)

In November 1941 7ᵗʰ Armoured Division instructions ordered that these RA symbols were to be grouped, with an 8" x 4" plate mounted directly above the "unit sign", e.g. the AOS plate. This was to be divided into two small 4x4 plates, the Offside (RHS) bearing the code for the vehicle, the Nearside (LHS) the battery indicator.

These 8" x 4" plates (without the AOS plate) could also be painted onto the sides of the vehicle if the unit desired.[14] It is not known how long this instruction remained in place, but it was in use with 5RHA on Sextons in Normandy in 1944. This featured a combination battery indicator with tactical number painted on it, above the formation sign, above the 76 AOS plate. This system, modified when necessary, remained in use until at least the late 1960s.

NON-STANDARD RA SYSTEMS

It is worth stressing that not all RA units followed this system in WW2, some preferring to use a system of geometric shapes containing callsigns in much the same way as used by the armoured regiments. And in some instances, both systems were used in the same unit at the same time. An M7 Priest in Normandy used a circular Battery Sign enclosing F4; this would appear to represent the 3rd Battery (circle) 6th Troop (F) 4th Gun (4). Another Priest had a light coloured solid triangle enclosing B2; this would be the 2nd gun in B Troop of the senior battery.

The BK of the 1st Battery in use post-war on an Austin Champ.

This callsign on this Priest in Tunisia indicates Gun 1 of G Tp, and thus the existence of a non-standard fourth Battery. However, the circle indicates the third battery, so it may be that in this case each Battery had three troops rather than two. (IWM NA2264)

149

POST WAR
GEOMETRIC SIGNS

Fourth Regiment in Brigade: B Sqn. (Left) and D Sqn. (Right)

432 of 1RTR in 1993, with the REME callsign 24A in a Yellow D Sqn rectangle; note the Chinese Eye that the First wore after amalgamation that year with the Fourth. (TM 4650/C/2)

Regulations issued in 1950 laid down the shapes and colours of sub-unit geometric signs for armoured formations and units. The HQ, A, B, C and D marks remained unchanged. The colour/seniority system was still used, with the first three Regiments/Battalions using the sequence Red-Yellow-Blue as before. The fourth senior unit in a formation, however, was to paint its signs in Red (left half) and Yellow (right half); the 'D' vertical bar sign was to be halved Red over Yellow. Motor Battalions were to use (presumably bright) Green, and un-brigaded units White. The 1959 version of the pamphlet was similar, but noted that the signs were to be used by all units other than the RA, and that "Troop, Platoon, Section and Tank numbers will be painted in the allotted colour inside or beside the signs."

The colour of Sqn geometric markings, and the callsigns painted within them, varied quite a lot from the 1970s onwards, with White, Yellow and Grey all being seen. This probably coincided with the introduction of the Green and Black scheme, and reflected a more tactically focused mindset in the army. Some units took camouflage to extremes with either Black on Green or Green on Black callsigns and symbols – almost impossible to see from more that a few yards away. When on gunnery ranges, these units had to make the callsigns more visible for safety reasons, and temporary metal plates fixed to turret rears were much used on firing camps and on exercises, with White on Black being the commonest colours used.

The fourth (D) sub-unit marking changed in the 1980s from the lazy D that had come into use in the 1950s to an open (stencilled) rectangle, containing the callsign. Many units disliked the rectangle, as it could be too easily confused with the B Sqn square. Lazy Ds were therefore sometimes used as before, but several units preferred an upside down triangle; D Sqn KRH in the move into Kosovo in 1999 used an inverted triangle with the C/S inside as their Sqn marking, and this was painted on the hull sides, as well as the turret sides and rear.

KOREAN WAR CALLSIGNS

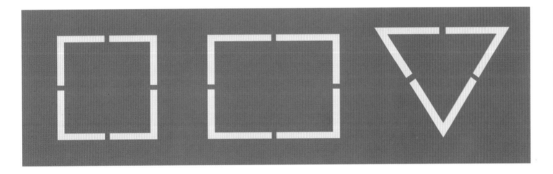

B Sqn. (Left) and
D Sqn alternatives.
(Centre and Right)

The 1980s system
- Landrover 43A
(Liaison Officer) in
UN service; this is the
B Sqn square symbol.
(TM 4643/D/2)

In Korea in 1950/51 8th Kings Royal Irish Hussars, and in 1951/52 5th Inniskilling Dragoon Guards, adopted the system shown below. 8 KRIH used a Black plate that was fixed towards the top of the centre of the bazooka plates, and also on the rear of the turret bustle. Superimposed upon it was a White Sqn tactical sign, within which, also in White, was a letter/number combination as follows:

Sqn Leader   - S
Sqn 2IC   - SA
SHQ tank   - SB

SHQ tank   - SC   2nd Tp   - 2 to 2C
1st Tp Ldr   - 1   3rd Tp   - 3 to 3C
1st Tp Sgt   - 1A   (It can be reasonably assumed, although
1st Tp Cpl   - 1B   positive evidence is lacking, that RHQ tanks
1st Tp LCpl   - 1C

belonging to the CO and 2IC would be marked R and RA.) 5 Inniskilling DG used the same system but within Red geometric squadron symbols.

CAPTAIN COTTLE a Centurion of SHQ C Sqn 8 KRIH in Korea with the callsign SB; note the Allied Star was partly obliterated by the later attachment of the callsign plate on a Black background. (TM 6254/C/2)

C Sqn 6RTR practicing beach landings before Suez in 1956; the Centurion appears to be using a recently applied regiment-specific callsign system. (Courtesy Paul Brewer MBE)

Recce Tp 3RTR in the 1950s – the R inside the HQ Sqn diamond denotes the troop but not the individual vehicle. (Courtesy David Buxton)

THE 1960s CALLSIGN SYSTEM

In the 1960s the callsign system that previously had been left to formations and units to design had been developed and standardised throughout the army, and which also included the Royal Marines and the RAF Regiment. A common basic structure was used regardless of the role of the unit, so callsign 9B was always the Adjutant, for example. Detailed below is the 1965 version of the main RAC elements of the system. Note that the symbol Ø had come into use for 'Zero', to avoid confusion with the letter 'O'. This symbol was almost invariably used thereafter when painting callsigns onto vehicles. Notice how the A, B, C etc suffix system was still used to designate subordinates in descending levels of seniority.

The 1960s system – A Centurion in Berlin with C/S 14A, thus A Sqn 4th Tp Sgt. (TM 1811/E/5)

153

ARMOURED REGT RHQ & HQ SQUADRON:

CALLSIGN	ROLE
ØA, ØB, ØC, ØD	RHQ Control Vehicles
9	CO (Softskin)
9A	Regt 2IC (Softskin)
9B	Adjt
9C	Sigs Offr
9D	Int Offr
9E	Liaison Offr
9F	RSM
91	QM
92	QM(T)
94	Medical Offr
94A	Ambulance
95	A1 Echelon

CALLSIGN	ROLE
95A	A2 Echelon
95B	B Echelon
96	Bridgelayer
98	OC LAD
98A	ASM
98B	LAD
88B	Recovery Tracked
88C	Recovery Wheeled
99	OC HQ Sqn
99A	2IC HQ Sqn
99F	SSM HQ Sqn
99H	SQMS HQ Sqn
99K-P	Spare Tanks

ARMOURED SQN

ROLE	A Sqn	B Sqn	C Sqn
OC MBT	1ØA	2ØA	3ØA
2IC MBT	1ØB	2ØB	3ØB
SHQ MBTs	1ØC, 1ØD	2ØC, 2ØD	3ØC, 3ØD
1st Tp Ldr	11	21	31
1st Tp Sgt	11A	21A	31A
1st Tp Cpl	11B	21B	31B
2nd Tp Ldr	12	22	32
2nd Tp Sgt	12A	22A	32A
2nd Tp Cpl	12B	22B	32B
3rd Tp Ldr	13	23	33
3rd Tp Sgt	13A	23A	33A
3rd Tp Cpl	13B	23B	33B
4th Tp Ldr	14	24	34

ROLE	A Sqn	B Sqn	C Sqn
4th Tp Sgt	14A	24A	34A
4th Tp Cpl	14B	24B	34B
Fitters	18, 18A	28, 28A	38, 38A
OC Softskin	19	29	39
2IC Softskin	19A	29A	39A
2ND CAPT	19B	29B	39B
LO	19E	29E	39E
SSM	19F	29F	39F
Dozer	19G	29G	39G
SQMS	19H	29H	39H
Ambulance	19J	29J	39J
A1 Ech	19K	29K	39K

ARMOURED REGT, RECCE SQN:

CALLSIGN	ROLE
4ØA, 4ØB, 4ØC, 4ØD	HQ Vehicles
41, 41A, 41B	Air Troop Helicopters
42, 42A, 42B, 42C	1 Tp Recce Vehicles

CALLSIGN	ROLE
43, 43A, 43B, 43C	2 Tp Recce Vehicles
44, 44A, 44B, 44C	3 Tp Recce Vehicles
5, 5A – 5E	GW Tp Vehicles

ARMOURED RECCE REGT, RECCE SQNS

ROLE	A Sqn	B Sqn	C Sqn
OC Vehicle	1ØA	2ØA	3ØA
2IC Vehicle	1ØB	2ØB	3ØB
SHQ Vehicles	1ØC, 1ØD	2ØC, 2ØD	3ØC, 3ØD
1st Tp Ldr	11	21	31
1st Tp Sgt	11A	21A	31A
1st Tp Cpl	11B	21B	31B
1st Tp 2nd Cpl	11C	21C	31C
2nd Tp Ldr	12	22	32
2nd Tp Sgt	12A	22A	32A
2nd Tp Cpl	12B	22B	32B
2nd Tp 2nd Cpl	12C	22C	32C
3rd Tp Ldr	13	23	33
3rd Tp Sgt	13A	23A	33A
3rd Tp Cpl	13B	23B	33B
3rd Tp 2nd Cpl	13C	23C	33C
4th Tp Ldr	14	24	34
4th Tp Sgt	14A	24A	34A

ROLE	A Sqn	B Sqn	C Sqn
4th Tp Cpl	14B	24B	34B
4th Tp 2nd Cpl	14C	24C	34C
5th Tp Ldr	15	25	35
5th Tp Sgt	15A	25A	35A
5th Tp Cpl	15B	25B	35B
5th Tp 2nd Cpl	15C	25C	35C
Support Tp Ldr	16	26	36
Support Tp	16A-E	26A-E	36A-E
Fitters	18	28	38
OC Softskin	19	29	39
2IC Softskin	19A	29A	39A
LO	19E	29E	39E
SSM	19F	29F	39F
SQMS	19H	29H	39H
Ambulance	19J	29J	39J
A1 Ech	19K	29K	39K

THE 1970s CALLSIGN SYSTEM

The versions used during the 1970s were based upon modifications to the previous system; detailed below are the main elements of the 1978 edition.

ARMOURED REGT RHQ & HQ SQUADRON:

CALLSIGN	ROLE	CALLSIGN	ROLE
ØA, ØB, ØC	RHQ Control Vehicles	82	QM(T)
ØD, ØE	Command MBTs	82A	RQMS(T)
9	CO (Softskin)	83	Medical Offr
9A	Regt 2IC (Softskin)	83A	Ambulance
9Ø	Formation (Division) Commander	84	MTO
91	Adjt	85	A1 Echelon
92	Sigs Offr	85A	A2 Echelon
93	Int Offr	85B	B Echelon
94	Liaison Offr	88	OC LAD
95	RSM	88A	ASM
95A	Provost Sgt	88B	Recovery Tracked
97	Forward Air Controller	88C	Recovery Wheeled
98, 98A	Rebroadcast vehicles	89	OC HQ Sqn
99	Task Force (Brigade) Commander	89A	2IC HQ Sqn
8A, 8B	HQ Sqn Control Vehicles	89C	SSM HQ Sqn
81	QM	89D	SQMS HQ Sqn

ARMOURED SQN

ROLE	A Sqn	B Sqn	C Sqn	D Sqn (where used)
OC's MBT	1A	2A	3A	4A
2IC's MBT	1B	2B	3B	4B
SHQ 3rd MBT (where used)	1C	2C	3C	4C
1st Tp Ldr	11	21	31	41
1st Tp Sgt	11A	21A	31A	41A
1st Tp Cpl	11B	21B	31B	41B
1st Tp 2nd Cpl (where used)	11C	21C	31C	41C
2nd Tp Ldr	12	22	32	42
2nd Tp Sgt	12A	22A	32A	42A
2nd Tp Cpl	12B	22B	32B	42B
2nd Tp 2nd Cpl (where used)	12C	22C	32C	42C
3rd Tp Ldr	13	23	33	43
3rd Tp Sgt	13A	23A	33A	43A
3rd Tp Cpl	13B	23B	33B	43B
3rd Tp 2nd Cpl (where used)	13C	23C	33C	43C
4th Tp Ldr	14	24	34	44
4th Tp Sgt	14A	24A	34A	44A
4th Tp Cpl	14B	24B	34B	44B
4th Tp 2nd Cpl (where used)	14C	24C	34C	44C
Forward Air Controller	17	27	37	47
Fitters	18	28	38	48
ARV	18A	28A	38A	48A
FV 434	18B	28B	38B	48B
OC	19	29	39	49
2IC	19A	29A	39A	49A
SSM	19C	29C	39C	49C
SQMS	19D	29D	39D	49D
LO	19E	29E	39E	49E
Ambulance	19F	29F	39F	49F

Note: Not all Regiments formed a 4th Squadron or used 4 Troops per Sqn

MEDIUM RECCE (SCORPION) SQN

ROLE	A Sqn	B Sqn
Command Vehicle 1	1A	2A
Command Vehicle 2	1B	2B
1st Tp Ldr	11	21
1st Tp Sgt	11A	21A
1st Tp Cpl	11B	21B
1st Tp 2nd Cpl	11C	21C
2nd Tp Ldr	12	22
2nd Tp Sgt	12A	22A
2nd Tp Cpl	12B	22B
2nd Tp 2nd Cpl	12C	22C
3rd Tp Ldr	13	23
3rd Tp Sgt	13A	23A
3rd Tp Cpl	13B	23B
3rd Tp 2nd Cpl	13C	23C
4th Tp Ldr	14	24

ROLE	A Sqn	B Sqn
4th Tp Sgt	14A	24A
4th Tp Cpl	14B	24B
4th Tp 2nd	14C	24C
Surveillance Tp	16, 16A – 16D	26, 26A – 26D
Forward Air Controller	17	27
Fitters	18	28
Recovery Tracked	18A	28A
Recovery Wheeled	18B	28B
OC Softskin	19	29
2IC Softskin	19A	29A
SSM	19C	29C
SQMS	19D	29D
LO	19E	29E
Ambulance	19F	29F

Note: Medium Recce Sqns were used at Formation level

CLOSE RECCE (SCIMITAR) SQN

ROLE	CALLSIGN
Command Vehicle 1	6A
Command Vehicle 2	6B
1st Troop	61, 61A – 61G
2nd Troop	62, 62A – 62G
3rd Troop	63, 63A – 63G
4th Troop	64, 64A – 64G
5th Troop	65, 65A – 65G
Forward Air Controller	67

ROLE	CALLSIGN
Recovery Lt Tracked	68
OC Softskin	69
2IC Softskin	69A
SSM	69C
SQMS	69D
LO	69E
Ambulance	69F

Note: Close Recce Troops were attached to the Division's Armoured Regiments. Where Armoured Regiments had their own Recce (4th) Sqn, the callsigns above were also used, but there were only 4 Troops, and these were usually mixed 4 Scorpion & 4 Scimitar.

Because of the possibility of exactly the same callsigns being used within a Brigade, for example two 'B' squadrons from different Regiments, a system of Arm Indicators were used, and which were sometimes painted on as the prefix to a callsign. (In BATUS they were always painted on for safety reasons.) The senior Regiment took the first shown, the primary, and the junior regiment the second, or alternative. The spare letter **X** was available to be used on the very rare occasions where there was a third similar sub-unit. Where there was no possibility of confusion, only one Arm Indicator was detailed. These were:

Infantry	I, K	RM Commando	C	RAOC	O
RAC	T, U[15]	RCT	D	RMP	P
RA	G, W	RAF Regt	H	REME	R
RE	E, F	RAF aircraft	L	R Signals	S
AAC	A	RAMC	M	Spare	X
Para	B	RN aircraft	N		

The 1970s system - Chieftain 21B of B Sqn, using a temporary metal plate attached to the rear turret basket. (TM 3922/D/2)

A Chieftain. (with Dozer Blade) of SHQ C Sqn 3RTR also in BATUS.

John Alsop and Andy Fisher in BATUS 1977 with the troop corporal's tank from 6 Tp B Sqn 3RTR.

The rarely seen Uniform arm indicator, here used in BATUS by C Sqn 3RTR – the other Squadron on the exercise were C Sqn 13th/18th Hussars.

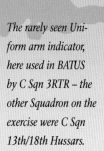

THE 1980s CALLSIGN SYSTEM

In the very early 1980s, a new system of callsigns was introduced. The intention was to stand-ardise callsigns in such a way that all types of unit, regardless of role, used the same basic matrix system, making interpretation of radio intercepts much harder. Furthermore, similar roles within the unit, regardless of level, used similar callsigns, with suffixes as necessary; thus the RSM was 33, and each SSM was 33A. ØA always represented the commander, whether of the Squadron or Regiment or Brigade. A grid system was used for this, with the Ø range (with suffixes) being used for the command/control stations and all others coming from a grid from 10 to 44, again with suf-fixes added from Alpha up to Delta (and where necessary further). To avoid confusion on the radio net where there were so many similar callsigns, a prefix letter (daily changing callsign indicator) was added to the callsign when speaking on the radio, but because they changed daily these were never marked on vehicles.[16] Two Support Groups were used, to allocate miscellaneous callsigns to Recce, Engineers, Aviation, Mortars, and Anti-Tank etc. A number of examples are shown below.

BATTLEGROUP/BATTALION/REGIMENT HQ

ØB CV1	ØC CV2	ØD CV3	ØE CV4
1Ø	2Ø	3Ø	4Ø
1ØA	2ØA	3ØA	4ØA
1ØB	2ØB	3ØB	4ØB
1ØC	2ØC	3ØC	4ØC
1ØD	2ØD	3ØD	4ØD
11	21 RSO	31 OC HQ	41 QM(T)
11A CO Landrover	21A RSWO	31A	41A RQMS(T)
11B CO AFV	21B	31B SSM HQ	41B
11C	21C	31C	41C
11D	21D Rebro	31D	41D
	21E Rebro		
	21F Rebro		
12	22 Regt 2IC	32	42 A2 Echelon CV
12A	22A Regt 2IC Landrover	32A	42A A1 Echelon CV
12B	22B Regt 2IC AFV	32B	42B B Echelon CV
12C	22C	32C	42C
12D	22D	32D	42D
13 MTO	23 QM	33 RSM	43 LO
13A MTWO	23A RQMS	33A Provost Sgt	43A LO
13B	23B SQMS HQ	33B	43B LO
13C	23C	33C	43C LO
13D	23D	33D	43D LO
14 MO	24	34	44
14A Ambulance	24A EME	34A	44A
14B Ambulance	24B ASM	34B	44B
14C	24C WR Recovery	34C	44C
14D Bde Comd	24D CRARRV	34D	44D
	24E Wheeled Recovery		
	24F 432		

Note: In all these tables, the users shown are those most likely to have their callsign actually marked on a vehicle; many other callsigns existed but are not shown. For instance, the Operations Officer was callsign 12, but would operate from Command Vehicle ØB, so it would be unusual to see an RHQ vehicle carrying the callsign 12.

ARMOURED SQN

ØB SHQ MBT1 (OC)	ØC SHQ MBT2 (2IC)	ØD SHQ MBT3 (SGT)	
1Ø 1 TP LDR	2Ø 1 TP LDR	3Ø 3 TP LDR	4Ø 4 TP LDR
1ØA	2ØA	3ØA	4ØA
1ØB	2ØB	3ØB	4ØB
1ØC	2ØC	3ØC	4ØC
1ØD	2ØD	3ØD	4ØD
11 1 TP SGT	21 2 TP SGT	31 3 TP SGT	41 4 TP SGT
11A OC Landrover	21A	31A	41A
11B	21B	31B	41B
11C	21C	31C	41C
11D	21D	31D	41D
12 1 TP CPL	22 2 TP CPL	32 3 TP CPL	42 4 TP CPL
12A	22A	32A	42A
12B	22B	32B	42B
12C	22C	32C	42C
12D	22D	32D	42D
13	23	33	43
13A	23A SQMS	33A SSM	43A LO
13B	23B	33B	43B LO
13C	23C	33C	43C
13D	23D	33D	43D
14 MO	24 LAD HQ	34	44
14A Ambulance	24A LAD 432	34A	44A
14B Ambulance	24B WR Recovery	34B	44B
14C	24C CRARRV	34C	44C
14D	24D	34D	44D

ARMOURED / MECHANISED INFANTRY COY

ØB COY HQ WR1 (OC)	ØC COY HQ WR2 (2IC)		
1Ø 1 PLN COMD	2Ø 2 PLN COMD	3Ø 3 PLN COMD	4Ø
1ØA	2ØA	3ØA	4ØA
1ØB	2ØB	3ØB	4ØB
1ØC	2ØC	3ØC	4ØC
1ØD	2ØD	3ØD	4ØD
11 1 PLN SGT	21 2 PLN SGT	31 3 PLN SGT	41
11A	21A	31A	41A
11B	21B	31B	41B
11C	21C	31C	41C
11D	21D	31D	41D
12 1 PLN CPL 1	22 2 PLN CPL 1	32 3 PLN CPL 1	42
12A	22A	32A	42A
12B	22B	32B	42B
12C	22C	32C	42C
12D	22D	32D	42D
13 1 PLN CPL 2	23 2 PLN CPL 2	33 3 PLN CPL 2	43
13A	23A CQMS	33A CSM	43A
13B	23B	33B	43B
13C	23C	33C	43C
13D	23D	33D	43D
14 MO	24 MT SGT	34	44
14A Ambulance	24A LAD WR	34A	44A
14B Ambulance	24B WR Recovery	34B	44B
14C	24C LAD 432	34C	44C
14D	24D LAD 432	34D	44D

SUPPORT GROUP 1

1Ø MORTAR PLN HQ	2Ø RECCE TP/PLN HQ	3Ø ATGW PLN HQ	4Ø ASLT PNR HQ
1ØA MOR PLN COMD	2ØA RECCE TP/PLN COMD	3ØA ATGW PLN COMD	4ØA ASLT PNR COMD
1ØB	2ØB	3ØB	4ØB
1ØC	2ØC	3ØC	4ØC
1ØD	2ØD	3ØD	4ØD
11 MORTAR SECT COMD	21 RECCE VEH TP LDR	31 ATGW SECT COMD	41
11A MORTAR	21A RECCE VEH	31A ATGW	41A
11B MORTAR	21B	31B ATGW	41B
11C MORTAR	21C	31C ATGW	41C
11D MORTAR	21D	31D ATGW	41D
		31E ATGW	
12 MORTAR SECT COMD	22 RECCE VEH TP SSGT	32 ATGW SECT COMD	42
12A MORTAR	22A RECCE VEH	32A ATGW	42A
12B MORTAR	22B	32B ATGW	42B
12C MORTAR	22C	32C ATGW	42C
12D MORTAR	22D	32D ATGW	42D
		32E ATGW	
13 MORTAR SECT COMD	23 RECCE VEH TP SGT	33 ATGW SECT COMD	43
13A MORTAR	23A RECCE VEH	33A ATGW	43A
13B MORTAR	23B	33B ATGW	43B
13C MORTAR	23C	33C ATGW	43C
13D MORTAR	23D	33D ATGW	43D
		33E ATGW	
14	24 RECCE VEH TP CPL	34 ATGW SECT COMD	44
14A	24A RECCE VEH	34A ATGW	44A
14B	24B	34B ATGW	44B
14C	24C	34C ATGW	44C
14D	24D	34D ATGW	44D
		34E ATGW	

SUPPORT GROUP 2

1Ø BTY COMD CV	2Ø HVM TP HQ	3Ø	4Ø AAC HQ
1ØA BTY COMD	2ØA HVM TP COMD	3ØA	4ØA AAC FLT COMD
1ØB	2ØB	3ØB	4ØB
1ØC	2ØC	3ØC	4ØC
1ØD	2ØD	3ØD	4ØD
11 FOO	21 HVM SECT 1 VEH1	31	41
11A	21A HVM SECT 1 VEH2	31A	41A
11B	21B HVM SECT 1 VEH3	31B	41B
11C	21C HVM SECT 1 VEH4	31C	41C
11D	21D	31D	41D
12 FOO	22 HVM SECT 2 VEH1	32	42
12A	22A HVM SECT 2 VEH2	32A	42A
12B	22B HVM SECT 2 VEH3	32B	42B
12C	22C HVM SECT 2 VEH4	32C	42C
12D	22D	32D	42D
13 FOO	23 HVM SECT 3 VEH1	33	43
13A	23A HVM SECT 3 VEH2	33A	43A
13B	23B HVM SECT 3 VEH3	33B	43B
13C	23C HVM SECT 3 VEH4	33C	43C
13D	23D	33D	43D
14 FOO	24 HVM SECT 4 VEH1	34	44
14A	24A HVM SECT 4 VEH2	34A	44A
14B	24B HVM SECT 4 VEH3	34B	44B
14C	24C HVM SECT 4 VEH4	34C	44C
14D	24D	34D	44D

ARMOURED ENGINEER SQN

1Ø	2Ø	3Ø	4Ø
1ØA	2ØA	3ØA	4ØA
1ØB	2ØB	3ØB	4ØB
1ØC	2ØC	3ØC	4ØC
1ØD	2ØD	3ØD	4ØD
11 ENGR RECCE	21 FD SECT	31 AVRE	41
11A ENGR RECCE	21A FD SECT	31A AVRE	41A
11B ENGR RECCE	21B FD SECT	31B AVRE	41B
11C ENGR RECCE	21C FD SECT	31C AVRE	41C
11D	21D	31D AVRE	41D
		31E AVRE	
12	22	32	42 CET
12A	22A	32A	42A CET
12B	22B	32B	42B CET
12C	22C	32C	42C CET
12D	22D	32D	42D CET
			42E CET
13	23 FD SECT	33 AVLB	43
13A	23A FD SECT	33A AVLB	43A
13B	23B FD SECT	33B AVLB	43B
13C	23C FD SECT	33C AVLB	43C
13D	23D	33D AVLB	43D
		33E AVLB	
14	24 BRIDGE	34	44 BRIDGE
14A	24A BRIDGE	34A	44A BRIDGE
14B	24B BRIDGE	34B	44B BRIDGE
14C	24C BRIDGE	34C	44C BRIDGE
14D	24D BRIDGE	34D	44D BRIDGE
			44E BRIDGE

ARMOURED RECCE SQN

1Ø 1 TP LDR	2Ø 2 TP LDR	3Ø 3 TP LDR	4Ø SP TP LDR
1ØA	2ØA	3ØA	4ØA
1ØB	2ØB	3ØB	4ØB
1ØC	2ØC	3ØC	4ØC
1ØD	2ØD	3ØD	4ØD
11 1 TP SGT	21 2 TP SGT	31 3 TP SGT	41 SP TP SGT
11A	21A	31A	41A
11B	21B	31B	41B
11C	21C	31C	11C
11D	21D	31D	41D
12 1 TP CPL 1	22 2 TP CPL 1	32 3 TP CPL 1	42 SP TP CPL 1
12A	22A	32A	42A
12B	22B	32B	42B
12C	22C	32C	42C
12D	22D	32D	42D
13 1 TP CPL 2	23 2 TP CPL 2	33 3 TP CPL 2	43 SP TP CPL 2
13A	23A SQMS	33A SSM	43A
13B	23B	33B	43B
13C	23C	33C	43C
13D	23D	33D	43D
14	24 LAD HQ	34 ATGW TP LDR	44
14A	24A LAD	34A ATGW TP SGT	44A
14B Ambulance	24B LAD	34B ATGW TP CPL1	44B
14C	24C LAD	34C ATGW TP CPL 2	44C
14D	24D LAD		44D

It can be immediately seen that a vehicle painted with the callsign 21 could be the Regimental Signals Officer, a Challenger Tp Sgt; a Warrior Pln Sgt; a Recce Tp/Pln leader; an HVM Section Comd; an RE Field Section Comd; or a Recce Sqn Tp Sgt! On radio nets the daily changing callsign indicator would distinguish them, whilst on the ground the vehicle type would be the main indicator.

22B inside the HQ diamond designates the Regimental 2IC. A lot of regiments chose to use the less visible but more tactical colours shown here. (Courtesy Richard Stickland)

B Coy. (or Sqn or Bty) 33A, therefore the CSM. (or SSM or BSM!)

B Sqn SHQ Challenger ZERO DELTA.

C Sqn 32 in Bosnia; note the white bands on the fume extractor identifying a 3 Tp tank. (Courtesy Richard Stickland)

4 Tp Leader in C Sqn 3RTR.

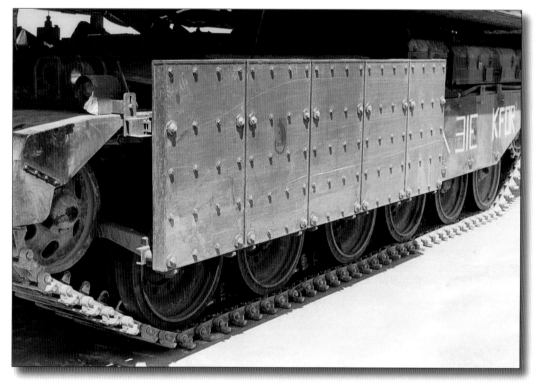

31E is officially an AVRE, but here in Kosovo the callsign is being used on an AVLB. Note the 7th Armd Bde Red rat. (Courtesy Richard Stickland)

Again, a strange callsign – CETs should use 42 series callsigns! The yellow symbol under the name JUNO appears to be from the flag of Ceylon, and the bucket sides have been painted either White or Light Grey. (Courtesy Richard Stickland)

Warriors of 1st Bn Staffords in Iraq in 1991.

IRAQ 2003

During OP TELIC in Iraq in 2003, 2RTR used a system of markings on the fume extractors of their Challenger 2s to denote troops. This was not new, as it had been in use by many armoured regiments for a number of years[17], but this example will serve for the whole system. The fume extractors were painted either Black or Light Stone. White or Black bands were marked on them; the number of bands (1-4) indicated the Troop number. The colours were:

– CYCLOPS (1st Sqn) Light Stone Fume Extractors with White Bands
– EGYPT (2nd Sqn) Black Fume Extractors with White Bands
– FALCON (3rd Sqn) Light Stone Fume Extractors with Black Bands

The individual tank callsign could be indicated by additional White bands on the muzzle, the troop leader having none, the troop Sgt one and the troop Cpl two. SHQ vehicles used the same colour fume extractors as the rest of the Sqn, but did not display any bands.

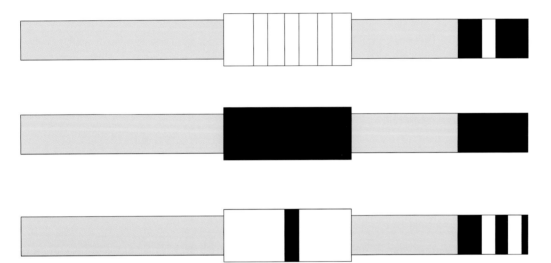

CYCLOPS 2RTR 3 Tp Sgt. (31).

EGYPT 2RTR SHQ Tank.

FALCON 2RTR 1 Tp Cpl. (12).

THE BATUS SUB-UNIT IDENTIFICATION SYSTEM

Identification of individual vehicles in BATUS was very important for two reasons: firstly for the usual tactical reason that vehicles had to be able to distinguish each other on the battlefield; and secondly, it was needed for range safety and control purposes. A number of complimentary systems were therefore used. The first of these was based upon the normal callsign system. Large white numbers, sometimes with letters as prefixes and/or suffixes, were painted prominently on black backgrounds on both sides and the rear of each vehicle. Locations differed according to vehicle type, with some minor variations noted within vehicle types. In general terms, vehicles without turrets had their callsigns on the hull sides, generally central, and also on a suitable location on the rear; often on a stowage bin. Turreted vehicles also had the callsigns repeated on the turret sides and rear (for when the turret was traversed off the centerline of the hull), but in the case of tanks did not have a callsign painted on the hull rear.

Because there were two squadrons of tanks and two companies of infantry, further distinguishing features were required. The first tank sqn had a vertical White stripe on the rear bazooka plate, and the main armament fume extractors on tanks were also painted White. The second armoured sqn and second infantry coy both had a White square outlining the Black callsign backgrounds. This table shows the system and locations as at 2003:

Vehicle Type	Sub-Unit	Callsign positions	Remarks
CR2	Armd Sqn 1	Turret sides,Turret rear (on NBC pack),Centre bazooka plates	White fume extractor. White vertical stripe on rear bazooka plate.
CR2	Armd Sqn 2	Turret sides,Turret rear (on NBC pack),Centre bazooka plates	Black fume extractor C/S outlined with white square.
CR2	Armd BG CO	As Armd Sqn 1	Uses C/S 11B
CR2	Armd BG 2IC	As Armd Sqn	Uses C/S 22B
Warrior	Armd Inf Coy 1	Turret sides,Turret rear , Centre hull side	
Warrior	Armd Inf Coy 2	Turret sides, Turret rear , Centre hull side	C/S outlined with white square
Warrior	FOO	Turret sides,Turret rear , Centre hull side	C/S starts with G eg G13.
Warrior	Inf BG CO	As Inf Coy 1	Uses C/S 11B
Warrior	Milan Pln	Turret sides,Turret rear , Centre hull side	C/S starts with W eg W32A.
AS90	Arty Gp		C/S starts with G eg G30C.
FV 432	All	Hull side central,Rear hull bin	Ambulances carry appropriate markings on all sides - position varies. Mortar Pln - C/S starts with M eg M12C.
CVR(T) Scorpion/Scimitar/Sabre	Recce	Turret sides,Turret rear , Centre hull side	
CVR(T) Spartan/Samson/Sultan	Various	Centre hull side,Hull rear	
HVM Stormer	HVM Tp		C/S starts with H eg H21A.
Armd Engineers	RE Sqn		C/S starts with E eg E31D.
B vehicles with radios	All	Side and rear of body	Engr, HVM etc vehicles use prefixes as above.
B vehicles without radios	All	Black background only - C/S not usually marked.	

It is worth noting that in BATUS, contrary to normal practice elsewhere, certain sub-units (Milan Pln, RA Bty, Mortar Pln, HVM Tp and the armoured engineers) have the callsign indicator prefixes noted in the table permanently painted onto the vehicles for easy identification.

A BATUS Bedford TM UBRE with the H indicator for the HVM Troop, Callsign 23E, the Zap number 581 and a plethora of legally required hazard stickers on the fuel tanks.

ENDNOTES:

1. When Tank Brigades were formed, these often ordered standardised practices to be used within the Brigade.
2. W/T represented Wireless Telegraphy (Morse), whilst R/T stood for Radio Telephony (Voice).
3. NA File WO/32/11617
4. Brigade or Division.
5. The seniority system was quite complicated. Each regiment held a position of seniority, but the type of unit also came into play. The order by type was: Household Cavalry; Line Cavalry Regiments (including the war-raised units, 22nd Dragoons to 27th Lancers); Regular RTR Battalions (1-12); Cavalry Militia (in the shape of one regiment only, The North Irish Horse); Yeomanry Cavalry (by seniority of the parent regiment); Territorial RTR Battalions (40-51); Infantry converted to armour (the RAC regiments). No wonder people got it wrong!
6. One instruction referred specifically to *Royal* Blue signs.
7. Southon papers, Tank Museum. Southon ended the war as a Major working on deception operations, and was consulted about camouflage matters, so he probably had a personal interest in the whole subject
8. Close *A View from the Turret* p 56
9. NA File WO 201/2795
10. Later in the war some serials as high as 31 were noted
11. 199/A4 was the vehicle that carried De Gaulle ashore.
12. 633/B19 was the vehicle that carried the King and Churchill ashore.
13. Sources here are often contradictory so it is unwise to be too dogmatic; however, a basic understanding of the system should assist in decoding some of the more esoteric variations.
14. NA File WO 201/2795
15. Only used by Tank equipped units
16. This in fact was very similar to RAC radio nets in 1944: on Regimental nets, each Sqn was allocated, on a daily basis, a Phonetic letter to be used as their callsign for that day. So A Sqn might be J (Jig), B Sqn W (William) and C Sqn B (Baker). Communication *within* the Sqn though only used the callsigns actually painted onto the tanks.
17. The Israeli armoured corps had been using the system – and recognition chevrons – for decades. It had also been previously used in the Gulf in 1991.

REFERENCES & BIBLIOGRAPHY

MUSEUMS LIBRARIES AND COLLECTIONS

The National Army Museum, London.
The Imperial War Museum, London.
The RAC & RTR Tank Museum and Library, Bovington, Dorset.
Firepower - The Royal Artillery Museum, Woolwich, London.
The Royal Engineers Museum and Library, Chatham, London.
The Royal Signals Museum, Blandford, Dorset.
The Museum of Army Flying, Middle Wallop, Hampshire.
The Staffordshire Regiment Museum, Lichfield, Staffordshire.
The Defence Intelligence and Security Centre Library, Chicksands, Bedfordshire.
The Mucklebrugh Collection, Norfolk.
The Museum of the Regiments, Calgary, Canada.

OFFICIAL MILITARY PUBLICATIONS & OTHER PRIMARY SOURCES - CHRONOLOGICAL

WO/5983 "*The Principles and Practice of Camouflage*" of Mar 1918
6061(QB8) "*Markings for Horse-Drawn and Motorised Vehicles*" 2nd June 1918
"*Tanks and their Employment in Co-operation with Other Arms*" August 1918
"*Light Armoured Motor Car Training Mesopotamia*" 1918
Tank Training Vol I "*Training and War*" 1920
Armoured Car Training: "*Training and War*" 1921
Tank and Armoured Car Training Vol II 1927 "*War.*"
Tank Training Vol I "*Training*" 1930
Armoured Car Training Vol II 1931 "*War.*"
Report on Training of 1st Army Tank Brigade 1932
Tank Training Vol II Part II "*Gunnery and Range Practices*" 1936
Signal Training All Arms 1938
Mobile Division Training Pamphlet No 2 1938 "*The Employment of the Tank Brigade.*"
Manual of Protection against Gas and Air Raids Pamphlet No 1 1939 "*Protection against Gas in the Field.*"
Military Training Pamphlet No 20 1939 "*Camouflage - Disruptive Painting of Vehicles.*"
Military Training Pamphlet No 26 1939 "*Notes on Concealment and Camouflage*"
ME GO 370 of 25 Jul 39 "*Painting of Vehicles*"
Field Service Pocket Book Pamphlet No3 "*Intelligence Information and Security*" 1939
Field Service Pocket Book Pamphlet No5 "*Billets Camps and Bivouacs*" 1939
Military Training Pamphlet No 27 "*Troop Training for Light Tank Troops*" 1939
WO 362.19 12 Jun 1940 "*Tactical Signs for Armoured Fighting Vehicle Units*"
AIF GS Instruction No 30 of 18 Nov 40 "*Vehicle Marking in War*".
AIF Admin Instruction No 8 of 25 Nov 40 "Tactical *Vehicle Marking of Vehicles*".
WO 57/Overseas/273 (AFV 1b) of 7 Dec 1940 "*Tactical Signs*"
9 Aust Div GS Instruction No 16 of 22 Feb 41 "*Vehicle Marking in War*".
HQ BF Palestine Memo of 14 Aug 41 "*Camouflage - Vehicles*".
Military Training Pamphlet No 46 1941 "*Camouflage Part 2: Field Defences*"
Military Training Pamphlet No 46 1941 "*Camouflage Part 4: Vehicles Wheeled and Tracked*"
Military Training Pamphlet No 46 1941 "*Camouflage Part 4A: Mechanical Transport, Artillery other than Anti-Aircraft*"

Military Training Pamphlet No 51 *"Troop Training for Cruiser Tank Troops"* 1941

ME Training Pamphlet No2 Part IA *"The Tactical Handling of the Armoured Regiment in the Middle East "*

ME Training Pamphlet No2 Part II *"Army Tank Brigades"* Oct 1941

ME Training Pamphlet No2 Part V *"Army Tank Brigade Operational Standing Orders"*

AFV Field Pocket Book 1942

Military Training Pamphlet No 10 (India) *Concealment and Camouflage Part 1* 1942

Military Training Pamphlet No 46 Supplement A 20 Oct 1943 *"Typical Layout of Standard Signs on WD Vehicles"*

Military Training Pamphlet No 46 Supplement B 20 Oct 1943 *"Typical Layout of Standard Signs on WD Vehicles"*

Military Training Pamphlet No 46 1942 : *"Camouflage Part 3: Huts, Camps and Installations"*

MELF GO 63 of 7 Feb 1941 *"Disruptive Patterning. (Guns and Vehicles)"*

AIF Mech Instruction No 10 of 6 Mar 1941 *"Camouflaging of Vehicles. (Egypt and Palestine)"*

MELF GO 795 of 8 Aug 1941 *"Camouflage of Artillery Equipment"*

GHQ MEF 4/105 of 6 Oct 1941 *"Camouflage Policy: Painting of Vehicles, AFVs and Artillery."*

MELF GO 1272 of 5 Dec 1941 *"Camouflage Painting of Vehicles, AFVs and Artillery Equipment"*

AIF Mech Instruction No 80 of 8 Jan 1942 *"Camouflage Painting of Vehicles"*

7 Aust Div AIF Memo of 17 Jan 42 *"Vehicle Marking in War"*

HQ AIF GS Instruction No 34 of Jan 42 *"Vehicle Marking in War"*.

9 Aust Div Admin Instruction No 67 of 29 Jan 42 *"Vehicle Markings"*.

CRME/38416/G(Cam)1 of 28 Feb 42 *"Camouflage Report No 1"*.

AIF GO 946 of 42 *"Camouflage – Painting of Vehicles"*

Gas Training India 1942

WO 201/2846 of Sep 1942 *"Notes on Vehicle Painting"*

British Standard 987C Sep 1942: *"Camouflage Colours"*

CRME/42497/G(Cam) of 19 Oct 1942 *"Instructions on Camouflage Painting of AFV's, Jeeps and Trucks"*

Military Training Pamphlet No 41 Part 2 Feb 1943: *"The Tactical Handling of the Armoured Division and its Components"*

WDR MISC 3264 *Camouflage of Artillery* G (CAM) HQ Eighth Army May 1943

Allied Forces HQ Camouflage Pamphlet No 1 May 1943 *"Concealment from the Air View"*

WO 465 of 20 Oct 1943 *"Vehicle Markings 1943"*

Gas Training India 1944

WO 57/Overseas/273 (AFV 1a) of 1 Mar 1944 *"Tactical Signs"*

Report on the RAC Conference 1945, 1947

Ministry of Supply Fighting Vehicles Proving Establishment Report No AT226 Pt VI June 1947 *"Camouflage Coating - British Zimmerit"*

Ministry of Supply Fighting Vehicles Design Department Feb 1948 *"FV Specification 2012 Painting of Fighting and Mechanical Transport Vehicles, Tracked and Wheeled"*

Regulations for the Equipment of the Army Pamphlet 5 1950 *"Markings of Vehicles"*

AP 3221A 1951 *"Gas Training "*

WO Code 9459 of 15 Nov 1959 *"Concealment in the Field"*

Equipment Regulations Pamphlet 9 1959 *"Markings and Painting of Vehicles, Army Aircraft and Equipment"*

Staff Duties in the Field Annex F 1962 *"Vehicle Unit Signs"*

RAC Training Armour Part 10 Apr 1965 : *"Tactical and Logistic Data"*

SCRDE Project No 686 of Jun 1970 *"Camouflage Painting of Vehicles and Equipment"*

Annex E to CRAOC Bulletin 8/77 *"Vehicles - Unit Identification Signs"*

Signal Communications Vol IV Pamphlet No 2 *Voice Procedure* Nov 1978

Material Regulations for the Army Vol 2 Pamphlet 3 Dec 1980 - *"Painting of Army Vehicles, Aircraft and Equipment"*

Catalogue of Ordnance Stores and Ammunition Section H1(a) 1983 *"Paints Dopes and Varnishes"*

Armoured Trials and Development Unit Report 8/0/4 of 31 Jul 1990 *"Standard Camouflage Paint Pattern"*

Joint Service Publication JSP327 *"Manual of Movements"* 1992

Army Field Manual Volume 1 Part 4 *"Counter Surveillance, Opsec and Deception"* 1999

Joint Service Publication JSP341 *"Defence Road Transport Regulations"* 2001

BATUS OPFOR Handbook 2003

British Standard 381C and RAL Colour Ranges (Courtesy Cromadex)

PUBLISHED REFERENCES – ALPHABETICAL BY AUTHOR

Ayliffe-Jones Noel (1984) *World Tanks and Reconnaissance Vehicles since 1945* Ian Allan
Beale Peter (1995) *Tank Tracks - 9th RTR in World War 2* Sutton
Beale Peter (1998) *Death by Design* Sutton
Bellis Malcolm A (1986) *The Divisions of the British Army 1939-45* Self Published
Bellis Malcolm A (1986) *The Brigades of the British Army 1939-45* Self Published
Bellis Malcolm A (2001) *The British Army Overseas 1945-1970* John Rigby
Bevis Mark (2001) *British & Commonwealth Armies 1939-43* Helion
Bevis Mark (2004) *British & Commonwealth Armies 1944-45* Helion
Birch Gavin (2005) *Sherman Tank* Pen & Sword
Bouchery Jean (2003) *The British Soldier Vol 2* Histoire & Collections
Brayley Martin (2001) *The British Army 1939-45 North West Europe* Osprey
Bruce Colin John (1995) *War on the Ground 1939-1945* Constable
Buffetaut Yves (1994) *D-Day Ships* Conway
Cabos Rodrigo and Prigent John (2001) *D-Day to Berlin* Osprey Publishing
Chamberlain Peter and Ellis Chris (1972) *Tanks of the World 1915-1945* Arms and Armour Press
Chamberlain Peter and Ellis Chris (2000) *British and American Tanks of World War II 1915-1945* Cassell
Chant Christopher (1996) *Artillery, Missiles & Military Transport* Tiger
Chappell Mike (2005) *British Battle Insignia 1* Osprey
Chappell Mike (2005) *British Battle Insignia 2* Osprey
Church John (1982) *Military Vehicles of World War 2* New Orchard Editions
Clarke Dale (2004) *British Artillery 1914-19* Osprey
Close Bill (1998) *A View from the Turret* Dell & Bredon
Cole Howard (1973) *Formation Badges of World War 2* Arms and Armour Press
Corrigan Gordon (2003) *Mud, Blood & Poppycock* Cassell
Crawford Steve (2000) *Tanks of WWII* Grange
Cunningham-Booth & Farrar Peter (Eds) (1988) *British Forces in the Korean War* BKVA
Daniels Peter & Sawyer Rex (1996) *Salisbury Plain* Chalford Publishing
Delaforce Patrick (1993) *Monty's Marauders* Chancellor Press
Delaforce Patrick (1996) *Marching to the Sound of Gunfire* Sutton Publishing
Delaforce Patrick (1999) *The Polar Bears* Chancellor Press
Delaforce Patrick (2000) *Taming the Panzers - 3RTR At War* Sutton Publishing
Delaforce Patrick (2001) *Churchill's Desert Rats* Chancellor Press
Delaforce Patrick (2001) *Monty's Iron Sides* Chancellor Press
Delaforce Patrick (2002) *The Fighting Wessex Wyverns* Sutton Publishing
Delaforce Patrick (2002) *The Black Bull* Sutton Publishing
Delaforce Patrick (2004) *Monty's Northern Legions* Sutton Publishing
Dunstan Simon (1989) *British Armoured Cars Since 1945* Arms and Armour Press
Dunstan Simon (1998) *Warrior Company* The Crowood Press
Dunstan Simon (1989) *Armour of the Korean War 1950-53* Osprey
Dunstan Simon (2003) *Chieftain Main Battle Tank 1965-2003* Osprey
Dunstan Simon (2003) *Centurion Universal Tank 1943-2003* Osprey
Ellis Chris & Chamberlain Peter (1976) *Handbook on the British Army 1943* Arms and Armour Press
Ellis Chris & Bishop Denis (1970) *Military Transport of World War I* Blandford
Ellis Chris & Bishop Denis (1971) *Military Transport of World War II* Blandford
Essame Maj Gen H (1952) *The 43rd Wessex Division at War* William Clowes
Fairfax Ernest (1945) *Calling All Arms* Hutchinson
Fletcher David (1984) *British Tanks in the First World War* HMSO

Fletcher David (1989) *The Great Tank Scandal* HMSO

Fletcher David (1990) *Staff Cars* Shire Publishing

Fletcher David (1991) *Mechanised Force: British Tanks Between The Wars* HMSO

Fletcher David (1995) *Crusader and Covenanter Tanks 1939-45* Osprey

Fletcher David (Ed) (1998) *Tanks and Trenches* Sutton Publishing

Fletcher David (1998) *British Military Transport 1829-1956* The Stationery Office

Fletcher David (2000) *British Tanks of WWII. (1) France & Belgium 1944* Concord

Fletcher David (2001) *British Tanks of WWII. (2) Holland & Germany 1944/1945* Concord

Fletcher David (2001) *The British Tanks 1915-1919* The Crowood Press

Fletcher David (2001) *Tanks in Camera 1940-1943* Sutton Publishing

Fletcher David (2003) *Matilda Infantry Tank 1938-45* Osprey

Fletcher David (2004) *British Mark I Tank 1916* Osprey

Fletcher David (2005) *Universal Carrier 1936-48* Osprey

Flint Keith (2004) *Airborne Armour* Helion

Foley CJ *ABC of British Army Vehicles* Ian Allan

Foley John (1967) *Armour in Profile No 1 - Tank Mk IV* Profile

Fortin Ludovic (2005) *British Tanks in Normandy* Histoire & Collections

Forty George (1979) *Chieftain* Ian Allan

Forty George and Forty Anne (1988) *Bovington Tanks* Dorset Publishing

Forty George (1995) *World War 2 Tanks* Osprey

Forty George (1998) *British Army Handbook 1939-1945* Sutton

Forty George (2001) *The Royal Tank Regiment* Halsgrove

Forty George (2003) *Spearhead: 7th Armoured Division* Arms and Armour Press

Foss Christopher (1984) *Light Tanks and Armoured Cars* Ian Allan

Gander Terry & Chamberlain Peter *Airfix Magazine Guide No 17 British Tanks of World War 2* Patrick Stephens

Gander Terry & Chamberlain Peter *Airfix Magazine Guide No 26 American Tanks of World War 2* Patrick Stephens

Glanfield John (2001) *The Devil's Chariots* Sutton

Gorman JT (1940) *The British Army* Collins

Grant Neil (1992) *The Illustrated History of 20th Century Conflict* Hamlyn

Graves Charles (1945) *Drive For Freedom* Hodder & Stoughton

Grove Eric (1978) *World War II Tanks* Orbis

Hawks Ellison (1941?) *Britain's Wonderful Fighting Forces* Odhams

Hills Stuart (2002) *By Tank Into Normandy* Cassell

Hodges Peter (1971) *British Military Markings 1939-1945* Almark

Hodges Peter and Taylor M (1994) *British Military Markings 1939-1945* Almark

Hogg Ian V (1973) *The Guns 1914-18* Pan Ballantyne

Hogg Ian V and Weeks John (1984) *The Illustrated History of Military Vehicles* Quanto

Hogg Ian V (2004) *Allied Artillery of World War One* Crowood

Holmes Richard (2004) *Tommy* Harper Collins

Horne Alistair (1995) *The Lonely Leader – Montgomery 1944-1945* Pan

Horsfall Jack & Cave Nigel (1999) *Cambrai: The Right Hook* Pen and Sword

Horsfall Jack & Cave Nigel (2002) *Bourlon Wood: Cambrai* Pen and Sword

Humphrys Julian (1994) *Monty's Men - The British Soldier and the D-Day Campaign* National Army Museum

Icks Robert (1967) *Armour in Profile No 16 - Carden Loyd Mk VI* Profile

Jane David (1978) *British Military Transport of World War 2* Almark

Jeffreys Alan (2003) *British Infantryman in the Far East 1941-45* Osprey

Jones Ken & Chamberlain Peter (1977) *Classic AFVs 2 Lee & Grant* Patrick Stephens

Jones Kenneth M (1977) *Focus on Armour Camouflage & Markings No 2 British North Africa* Almark

Joslen Lt Col HF (1990) *Orders of Battle Second World War 1939-1945* HMSO

Laber Thomas (1991) *British Army of the Rhine* Concord

Leakey Rea (with Forty George) (1999) *Leakey's Luck* Sutton

Lloyd Mark (1997)*The Art of Military Deception* Leo Cooper

MacDonald Lyn (1991) *Voices and Images of the Great War* Penguin

Macksey Ken (1970) *Tank Force: Allied Armour in the Second World War* Pan/Ballantine

Macksey Kenneth (1988) *Tank Versus Tank* Bantam

Masters David (1943) *With Pennants Flying* Eyre & Spottiswoode

McNish Robin (2000) *Iron Division - The History of the 3rd Division 1809-2000* Ian Allan

Messenger Charles (2003) *World War I in Colour* Ebury

Messenger Charles (2006) *Call To Arms The British Army 1914-18* Cassell

Miller David (2002) *The Great Book of Tanks* Salamander

Milsom John, Sandars John and Scarborough Gerald (1976) *Classic AFVs 1 Crusader* Patrick Stephens

Mitchell F (1935) *Tank Warfare* Naval & Military Press

Moore William (1991) *Panzer Bait - With the 3rd Royal Tank Regiment 1940-44* Leo Cooper

Ness Leland (2002) *Jane's World War II Tanks and Fighting Vehicles* Collins

Orchard CJ & Madden SJ (1995) *British Forces Motorcycles 1925-45* Sutton

Perrett Bryan (2000) *Iron Fist* Cassell

Pimlott John (Ed) (1984) *British Military Operations 1945-1984* Guild

Pidgeon Trevor (2002) *Flers & Gueudecourt* Leo Cooper

Pullen Richard (2003) *The Landships of Lincoln* Tucann

Ray David (2001) *The Western Front - A Pictorial History* Caxton

Rosse and Hill E *The Story of the Guards Armoured Division* Geoffrey Bles

Rosignoli Guido (1974) *Army Badges & Insignia of World War 2* Blandford

Smith RE (1968) *British Army Vehicles and Equipment* Ian Allan

Smithers AJ (1988) *A New Excalibur* Grafton

Smurthwaite David et al (1989) *Against All Odds - The British Army of 1939-40* National Army Museum

Stanley Roy M (1998) *To Fool a Glass Eye: Camouflage Versus Photo-Reconnaissance in WWII* Airlife

Starmer Mike (2003) *The Caunter Scheme* (Self Published)

Starmer Mike (2003) *Alamein and After 1942-1943* (Self Published)

Starmer Mike (2003) *Sicily and Italy 1943-1945* (Self Published)

Starmer Mike (2005) *British Army Colours & Disruptive Camouflage in the United Kingdom, France & NW Europe 1936-45* (Self Published)

Suermondt Jan (2001) *World War II Allied Vehicles* Crowood

Sutton DJ (Ed) (1984) *The Story of the RASC and the RCT 1945-1982* Leo Cooper

Sutton J & Walker J (1990) *From Horse to Helicopter* Leo Cooper

Thers Alexander (2004) *Armor in Normandy The British Tanks* Histoire & Collections

Tout Ken (1989) *Tanks, Advance!* Grafton

Upton Peter (1997) *The Cherrypicker* Private

Various (1920) *The Royal Artillery War Commemoration Book* Bellis & Sons

Various (1924) *Army Corps and Divisional Signs 1914-1918* John Player (Cigarette Cards)

Various (1940) *Badges and Emblems of the Services* NAG Press

Various (1943) *The Eighth Army* HMSO

Various (1990) *Against All Odds: The British Army of 1939-40* NAM

Various *Mechanisation of the British Army of 1919-1939-40* IWM

Wheeler-Holohan V (1920) *Divisional and Other Signs* Naval & Military Press

White BT (c1970) *British Tanks 1915-1945* Ian Allan

White BT (1970) *British Tanks and Fighting Vehicles 1914-1945* Ian Allan

White BT (1975) *Tanks and other Armoured Fighting Vehicles of World War II* Peerage

White BT (1978) *British Tank Markings and Names* Arms and Armour Press

Wilson Edward (2003) *Press On Regardless - 5th RTR in World War 2* Spellmount

Windrow Martin (2003) *Tank and AFV Crew Uniforms Since 1916* Patrick Stephens

Wise Terence (1971) *Military Vehicle Markings* Bellona

Wise Terence (1973) *Military Vehicle Markings 2* Bellona

Wise Terence (1995) *D-Day to Berlin* Arms and Armour Press
Zaloga Steven J(1980) *Blitzkrieg - Armour Camouflage and Markings 1939-40* Guild
Zaloga Steven J & Balin George (1994) *Tank Warfare in Korea 1950-53* Concord

MAGAZINES AND PERIODICALS – ALPHABETICAL BY TITLE

Airfix Magazine
Classic Military Vehicles - Kelsey Publishing
Military Illustrated - Publishing News Ltd
Military Machines International - Tony Dowdeswell Publishing
Military Modelcraft International - Tony Dowdeswell Publishing
Military Modelling - Highbury Leisure Publishing
Soldier - The Magazine of the British Army
Tank - The Journal of the Royal Tank Regiment
Tankette - The MAFVA Journal
The Dragon – The MAFVA South Wales Newsletter
The Fight for Iraq - London, MOD
War Monthly - Marshall Cavendish Publishing

INTERNET RESOURCES - ALPHABETICAL

www.armouredacorn.com
www.armourinfocus.co.uk
www.awm.gov.au
www.britisharmedforces.org
www.britishpathe.com
www.ferretscoutcar.info
www.firepower.org.uk
www.fleetdata.co.uk
www.irishmilitaryinsignia.com
www.iwmcollections.org.uk
www.landships.freeservers.com
www.lightinfantry.org.uk
www.mafva.org
http://milifax2003.tripod.com
www.missing-lynx.com
www.mod.uk
www.nationalarchives.gov.uk
www.ra39-45.pwp.blueyonder.co.uk
www.1914-1918.net/.htm

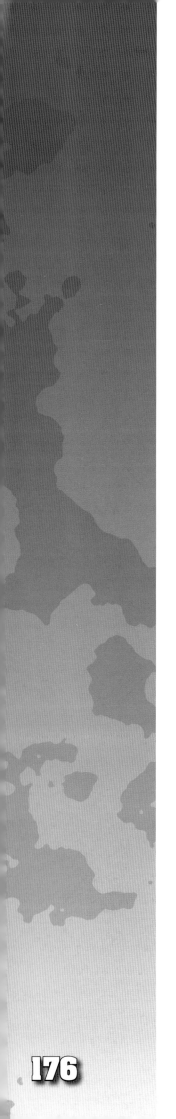